Chapter One

Christmas Day

Dave stood in his living room on Christmas afternoon, holding a gift voucher and trying to look grateful.

"It's like tennis but in a cage," his brother-in-law explained, gesturing vaguely with a Quality Street. "Very big in Spain. There's a new court at that leisure centre near you. ActiveLife, I think?"

"Oh, brilliant. Thanks mate." Dave smiled the smile of someone who has absolutely no intention of using something.

Sarah, his wife, looked up from wrapping paper carnage. "You're always saying you need to get more exercise."

"Yeah... definitely. Thanks, Rob. Really thoughtful."

It was thoughtful. Rob was good at gifts. Last year he'd given Dave a book about decluttering that Dave had read twice and implemented exactly never. The year before, a "craft gin experience" that had resulted in Dave discovering he preferred normal gin.

This year: **"Padel Experience - 2 Free Sessions at ActiveLife Leisure Centre"**

Dave turned the voucher over. There was a photo of four people in a glass-walled court, holding what looked like oversized table tennis bats, all grinning like they'd discovered the meaning of life. One of them was mid-jump. Nobody in their right mind should be that enthusiastic about exercise.

"What even is Padel?" Dave's daughter Emily asked from the sofa, not looking up from her phone.

"It's like squash but outside," Rob said confidently.

"I thought you said tennis?" Dave's son Tom pointed out.

"Well, yeah. Tennis crossed with squash. Spanish thing. Apparently it's massive over there."

"So is bullfighting," Emily muttered.

Dave's sister-in-law Linda laughed. "To be fair, Rob's been going for a few months. He won't shut up about it."

"I don't go on about it," Rob protested.

"You literally have a Padel paddle in your car."

"That's just practical. In case anyone wants to—"

"You wore your Padel top to my mum's birthday."

"It's moisture-wicking!"

You Play Padel? Funny, You Never Mentioned It!

A Tale of Middle Age Obsession
Ariel Wisherty

Contents

Dave caught Sarah's eye. She was smiling in that way that meant she was storing this information for later mockery.

The afternoon continued its predictable rhythm. Cheese board. Pointless on TV. Tom's girlfriend Megan arrived, was offered seventeen different types of chocolate, accepted a Ferrero Rocher. Emily's boyfriend was spending Christmas with his own family, which Emily claimed to be "totally fine about" while refreshing Instagram every forty seconds.

Dave's mum asked if anyone wanted more turkey. Nobody did. They all had some anyway.

By 6pm, the house had that specific Christmas Day atmosphere - too warm, too full, everyone slightly uncomfortable but nobody wanting to be the first to leave. The Morecambe and Wise Christmas special played on TV. Everyone had seen it before. Everyone watched anyway.

Dave found himself staring at the Padel voucher, which he'd propped against a empty Quality Street tin on the coffee table.

"You should do it," Sarah said, appearing beside him with two mugs of tea. "The Padel thing."

"Yeah, maybe."

"I'm serious. When was the last time you did proper exercise?"

Dave thought about this. "I walked to the shop on Tuesday."

"For chocolate digestives."

"Still counts."

"Dave. You're forty-seven. Your idea of cardio is taking the stairs at work instead of the lift, and you only do that when you've just eaten lunch and feel guilty."

This was accurate.

"I just don't know if Padel is really... me," Dave said.

"What, fun?" Sarah sat down next to him. "When did you get old?"

"I'm not old."

"You spent last Saturday alphabetising the spice rack."

"It needed doing! How are you supposed to find anything when the cumin is next to the—"

"Dave. Use the voucher. Or at least don't spend the next six months feeling guilty about not using it, which is definitely what you'll do otherwise."

She was right. That was exactly what he'd do. The voucher would live in the drawer in the kitchen with the instruction manuals and loose batteries and that key that definitely unlocked something important but nobody could remember what. Every time Dave opened the drawer, he'd see it. Feel guilty. Close the drawer. Repeat.

"Fine," Dave said. "I'll give it a go."

"Good." Sarah patted his knee and stood up. "I'm going to make sure your mum isn't overfeeding the dog again."

Dave picked up his phone. Then put it down. Then picked it up again.

It was 6:47pm on Christmas Day. Everyone was full of food and regret. This was not the time to be investigating sporting activities.

He opened Google anyway.

"What is Padel?" he typed.

The search results loaded. Dave scrolled. Clicked a video. A Spanish man in very tight shorts was explaining something in Spanish with English subtitles. Dave watched for thirty seconds, understood approximately nothing, clicked another video.

This one was in English. Two enthusiastic Australians demonstrating technique. They kept saying "mate" and "beautiful" and making it look very easy. Dave was suspicious of people who made things look easy.

He clicked another video. And another. By 7:15pm he'd watched seventeen Padel videos and was developing strong opinions about grip technique.

"Everything alright?" Sarah appeared in the doorway.

Dave jumped slightly, closing YouTube quickly as if he'd been caught watching something he shouldn't.

"Fine! Just looking at that Padel thing."

"For the last half hour?"

Had it been half hour? Dave checked the time. It had been forty-five minutes.

"Just wanted to understand what it was before I, you know, turned up."

Sarah smiled that smile again. The one that meant she knew something he didn't know yet.

"Well?" she asked. "What do you think?"

"Looks... interesting," Dave admitted. "Quite technical. Lots of spin. The walls are in play, which adds a tactical element. And apparently the serve has to be underarm, which is unusual. Also there's something called a 'bandeja' which is like a defensive overhead but—" He stopped. Sarah was grinning. "What?"

"Nothing. I'm just pleased you're interested in something."

"I'm not that interested. I just thought I should research it properly."

"Of course. Very sensible." She turned to go, then paused. "Your brother-in-law Rob was exactly like this. Three YouTube videos and suddenly he was buying a paddle."

"I'm not buying a paddle."

"Good. Just checking." She disappeared back into the kitchen.

Dave looked at his phone again. There was a notification. A Facebook memory from seven years ago: Dave and Tom at the driving range, both mid-swing, both terrible. The caption read: "Quality father-son time! I'm definitely getting better at this!"

He hadn't been to the driving range since.

When had that happened? When had he become someone who didn't do things?

Dave opened his messages and scrolled to Mike Harrison. They'd been mates at school, lost touch for twenty years, reconnected at a mutual friend's fortieth about eight months ago. Since then they'd exchanged occasional messages - mostly "we should grab a pint" followed by neither of them actually grabbing a pint.

The last message was from Mike in November: "Fancy the football Saturday? Got a spare ticket."

Dave had said he was busy. He hadn't been busy. He'd just felt like staying home.

Dave typed: "Fancy trying something ridiculous? Got a free Padel voucher. No idea what it is. Looks like tennis for people who can't be bothered with proper courts."

He hovered over send for approximately fifteen seconds, then pressed it before he could change his mind.

The reply came back within two minutes.

"Padel! Mate I've been wanting to try that. When?"

Dave blinked at the screen. That was easier than expected.

"Not sure. Voucher's for ActiveLife. Need to book apparently."

Three dots appeared. Disappeared. Appeared again.

"I'll check their website. Been meaning to do something about the dad bod situation. Wife's been making comments."

"Same. Well, about the exercise. Sarah thinks I'm getting old."

"Are we getting old?"

"I alphabetised my spice rack last weekend."

"Fuck."

"I know."

"Right. I'm booking us in. New Year New Us and all that bollocks."

"Sounds horrific."

"Exactly. First week of January?"

"Go on then."

Dave put his phone down. Then picked it up again and Googled "what equipment do you need for Padel."

By 10pm he'd watched thirty-seven more videos, read four blog posts, and understood considerably less than when he'd started. Everyone had different opinions. Some people said you needed special shoes. Other people said trainers were fine. Some people said you should rent a paddle first. Others said you'd never improve without your own.

Dave made notes in his phone. Then organised the notes into categories. Then created a new note called "Padel Research" and transferred everything across with proper headings.

Sarah appeared in the doorway in her pyjamas.

"Coming to bed?"

"Yeah, just finishing something."

"Padel research?"

"Might be."

She smiled, kissed the top of his head. "Don't stay up too late Googling grip techniques."

"I won't."

He absolutely did.

By 11:30pm, Dave had learned that:

Padel was invented in Mexico in 1969

The court is 10x20 metres

You can only serve underarm

The back walls are glass, the side walls are either glass or mesh

Spanish people are really, really good at it

British people on YouTube are less good at it but very enthusiastic

There was something called "vibora" which was apparently crucial

Paddles came in three shapes: round, teardrop, or diamond

This somehow affected your playing style

Dave needed to pick a shape

This felt like an unreasonable amount of pressure for 11:30pm on Christmas Day

He closed YouTube and stared at the ceiling.

In the next room, Sarah was definitely asleep. Downstairs, someone - probably Emily - was in the kitchen making tea. The house creaked in that way houses do at night. The heating had turned itself off. Tomorrow they'd all have leftover turkey sandwiches and Quality Street for breakfast.

Dave opened YouTube again.

Just one more video.

Just to be sure.

By the time he finally went to bed at 12:15am, Dave had watched fifty-three Padel videos, joined two Facebook groups ("UK Padel Community" and "Padel Addicts Anonymous" - the second one he assumed was ironic), and saved seventeen different paddles to an Amazon wishlist he'd titled "Maybe?"

He had also messaged Mike three more times with "crucial information" about court positioning.

Mike had replied: "Mate. It's midnight. We haven't even played yet."

Dave had replied: "Just want to be prepared."

Which was sensible. Dave was always prepared. That's what made him good at his job. IT Project Manager. Planning was literally what he did.

He lay in bed, Sarah breathing steadily beside him, and thought about Padel.

Just thinking.

Not obsessing.

Definitely not obsessing.

At 2am he woke up having dreamed about doubles strategy.

He reached for his phone to make notes, then caught himself.

"This is ridiculous," he whispered to nobody.

Then made the notes anyway.

Just in case.

Chapter Two
The First Session

The ActiveLife Leisure Centre smelled exactly like every leisure centre Dave had ever been to: chlorine, rubber flooring, and that specific brand of optimism that came with January gym memberships.

It was the second Saturday in January. Dave and Mike stood in the reception area, both wearing clothes they'd described to their wives as "suitable for sport" but which more accurately could be described as "things we found in the back of the wardrobe that weren't actively embarrassing."

Dave had on his "good" tracksuit bottoms (only two years old, minimal bobbling), a t-shirt from a company away-day in 2019, and his regular trainers. Mike was wearing football shorts from his teenage son's abandoned kit and a polo shirt that had definitely shrunk in the wash.

"We look ridiculous," Dave said.

"Mate, we haven't even started yet. Save that energy for when we're actually playing."

The receptionist, a young woman with the kind of enthusiasm that suggested either genuine love of her job or exceptional acting skills, beamed at them. "Here for Padel?"

"That's us," Mike confirmed.

"Brilliant! First time?"

"Is it that obvious?" Dave asked.

"You've got that look. Don't worry, everyone's nervous their first time. The courts are through those doors, down the corridor, turn left. You're on Court 2. Your other two players are already there."

Dave and Mike looked at each other.

"Other two players?" Dave said.

The receptionist checked her screen. "Yeah, it's doubles. You're booked as a pair, but we've matched you with another pair. Standard for beginners' sessions. Makes it more fun!"

She said this with the confidence of someone who had never been forced into sporting activities with strangers.

"Right," Mike said. "Great. Strangers. Love that."

They collected their rental paddles - which looked, Dave thought, like someone had taken a table tennis bat, made it slightly bigger, and then decided holes were fashionable - and headed through the doors.

The corridor was lined with motivational posters. "PUSH YOUR LIMITS!" one shouted, next to a photo of someone doing a plank. "BE YOUR BEST SELF!" another insisted, featuring a woman mid-burpee who looked like she was having the time of her life.

"Do you think anyone's ever been inspired by these?" Dave asked.

"I'm inspired to leave," Mike muttered.

Court 2 was at the end of the corridor. Through the glass walls, they could see two men already warming up. One was tall, wearing proper sports gear - the kind with logos and moisture-wicking properties. The other was shorter, stockier, wearing what looked like five-a-side kit.

"They look like they know what they're doing," Dave observed.

"They probably just watched more YouTube videos than you."

"Nobody watched more YouTube videos than me."

They pushed through the door into the court.

The first thing Dave noticed was the walls. Glass at the back, wire mesh at the sides, all of it enclosing what felt like a surprisingly small space. The second thing he noticed was the heat. January outside, but the court was warm, almost humid.

The third thing he noticed was that both men had stopped warming up and were looking at them.

"Alright!" the tall one said. "You two the beginners' booking?"

"That's us," Mike said. "Mike and Dave."

"Rich. This is Steve." Rich gestured to the shorter man, who nodded. "First time?"

"Is it that obvious?"

"Mate, you're holding the paddles upside down."

Dave looked at his paddle. Then looked at how Rich was holding his. Then quietly rotated his paddle the right way up.

"Right," Dave said. "Obviously."

Steve grinned. "Don't worry about it. We've all been there. Well, not Rich. Rich showed up to his first session with his own paddle and a YouTube highlights reel."

"It's called being prepared," Rich said.

"It's called being a show-off."

There was an easy familiarity between them that suggested they'd known each other a while. Dave felt a small pang of something - not quite envy, but close to it. When was the last time he'd had that kind of casual friendship?

"So how does this work?" Mike asked. "I mean, we know the basic rules. Serve underarm, walls are in play, all that. But in practice..."

"Right, okay." Rich moved to the baseline. "Easiest way is to just start. Dave, you come over here with me. Mike, you're with Steve. We'll do some gentle rallies, get a feel for it."

They took their positions. Dave stood on the right side of the court, paddle gripped so tightly his knuckles were white.

"Relax your grip a bit," Rich said quietly. "You're not trying to strangle it."

Dave loosened his grip marginally.

Rich served. A gentle underarm lob that bounced once then hit the back glass. Dave watched it come off the glass, calculated the angle, positioned himself, swung—

And missed completely.

The ball bounced past him and rolled to the side wall.

"That's alright!" Rich called. "The glass takes getting used to. Try again."

They tried again. And again. By the fifth serve, Dave had managed to make contact with the ball. It went approximately three feet before dying with all the enthusiasm of a punctured balloon.

"Progress!" Rich said, and he seemed to mean it.

On the other side of the court, Mike was having similar success. Which is to say, very little success. Steve was being patient, encouraging, and definitely trying not to laugh.

After ten minutes of what could generously be called "rallies," Rich suggested they try an actual game.

"Nothing serious," he said. "Just first to eleven points. Get a feel for the scoring."

What followed could only be described as carnage.

Dave served. The ball hit the net. He served again. The ball went wide. Third serve went long. Fourth serve finally made it over, and Steve returned it directly into the wire mesh.

"Point to us!" Mike said triumphantly.

They did not score another point for seven minutes.

Rich and Steve were trying to keep the ball in play, Dave could tell. They weren't smashing it or going for winners. They were hitting gentle returns, aiming for the middle of the court, giving Dave and Mike every opportunity to return it.

Dave and Mike were returning approximately none of them.

The problem, Dave realised, was that everything he'd learned on YouTube was completely useless in practice. His brain knew what to do. His body had other ideas. The ball would come toward him, he'd position himself, prepare to hit it, and then at the last second everything would malfunction. He'd swing too early or too late or at the wrong angle or with the wrong amount of force.

At one point he hit the ball straight up. It went about fifteen feet in the air, came down, bounced three times, and rolled to a stop at his feet. Everyone stood in silence for a moment.

"Technical difficulties," Dave said.

By the time they finished the first game (11-2, and Dave suspected Rich and Steve had let them have those two points out of pity), Dave was sweating more than he'd sweated in possibly a decade. His t-shirt was stuck to his back. His trainers, which he'd thought were perfectly adequate, had exactly zero grip on the court surface. He'd nearly fallen over four times.

Mike looked similarly destroyed. His face was red. His hair was plastered to his forehead. He was breathing like he'd just run a marathon.

"Water break?" Steve suggested.

"God yes," Mike gasped.

They collapsed onto the bench at the side of the court. Dave had brought a water bottle. It was now empty. He'd drunk the entire thing in about forty seconds.

"So," Rich said, sitting down next to them, barely out of breath, "what do we think?"

Dave and Mike looked at each other.

"That was horrible," Dave said.

"Absolutely awful," Mike agreed.

"I think I've discovered muscles I didn't know I had," Dave continued. "And they're all angry about it."

"I hit myself in the face with my own paddle," Mike added.

"Twice," Steve pointed out.

"Twice," Mike confirmed. "The second time was worse because I knew it was coming."

There was a pause. Rich and Steve were clearly waiting for them to say they'd had enough, that this wasn't for them, that they'd stick to their normal routines of doing essentially nothing.

"Same time next week?" Dave asked.

Mike nodded immediately. "Absolutely."

Rich grinned. "Yeah?"

"Are you kidding?" Dave said. "I need to redeem myself. That was embarrassing. I can't end on that performance. I need at least one session where I don't look like I've never seen a ball before."

"Plus," Mike added, "I've already told Clare I'm doing this regularly now. If I quit after one session she'll never let me hear the end of it."

"Fair enough." Rich stood up. "You two want to go again? We've got the court for another forty minutes."

They went again.

The second game was marginally less disastrous than the first. Dave managed to return three balls in a row at one point. Mike successfully served without hitting the net. Small victories, but victories nonetheless.

By the end of the session, they'd lost three games, scored a combined total of eight points, and Dave had a blister forming on his right hand.

They were also both grinning like idiots.

In the changing rooms afterwards, peeling off their damp t-shirts and trying to convince their legs to work properly, they ran into Rich and Steve again.

"Good first session," Rich said, pulling on what Dave now recognised as obviously expensive sportswear. Everything matched. Everything had logos. Everything looked like it cost more than Dave's entire outfit combined.

"We were terrible," Dave said.

"Yeah, but you were enthusiastically terrible. That's the main thing."

"I didn't know there were levels of terrible," Mike said.

"Oh mate, there are loads." Steve was stuffing his kit into a worn Adidas bag. "Reluctantly terrible, apologetically terrible, angrily terrible. Enthusiastically terrible is the best kind. Means you'll actually improve."

"You two doing this regularly then?" Rich asked.

"Planning to," Dave said. "Assuming we can get bookings. The receptionist said courts fill up fast."

"Tell me about it. I've started setting alarms for midnight so I can book exactly seven days in advance."

"Midnight?" Mike said. "That's insane."

"Welcome to Padel," Steve said. "Where grown men set alarms for midnight to book sports courts."

There was something appealing about that, Dave thought. The shared madness of it. The commitment to something that was, objectively, quite silly.

"We should swap numbers," Rich suggested. "Make a WhatsApp group. Easier to coordinate bookings and stuff."

"You know what," Mike said, pulling out his phone, "that's actually sensible."

They exchanged numbers. Mike, who was apparently taking his organisational role seriously, created the group immediately.

"What should we call it?" he asked.

"Padel Lads?" Steve suggested.

"Bit obvious," Rich said.

"Terrible Tennis?" Dave offered.

"It's not tennis," Mike said.

"That's the joke."

"I know, but it'll confuse people."

"What people? Who's going to see this besides us?"

"Just future-proofing."

They settled on "Padel Lads " because Mike found a tennis ball emoji and nobody could be bothered to point out the irony.

The first message in the group came from Rich within seconds: "Same time next week?"

Three thumbs-up emojis appeared immediately.

Dave drove home in a pleasant daze. His legs ached. His shoulder hurt. His hand throbbed where the blister was forming. Everything smelled of sweat.

He felt fantastic.

Sarah was in the kitchen when he got home, chopping vegetables with the kind of precision that suggested she was planning something elaborate for dinner.

"How was it?" she asked, not looking up.

"Terrible," Dave said, filling a pint glass with water and drinking half of it in one go. "Absolutely awful. I was dreadful. We lost every game. I think I scored two points total."

"So you're not going again?"

"Next Saturday. Same time. Already booked."

Sarah looked up, smiling. "Yeah?"

"Yeah. I mean, I can't be that bad forever, can I? Law of averages suggests I have to improve eventually."

"That's not how the law of averages works."

"Well, law of something then. Law of... practice."

"That's called practice."

"Exactly."

Dave headed upstairs for a shower, his phone already buzzing with WhatsApp notifications. Mike had sent a gif of someone falling over. Steve had replied with a crying-laughing emoji. Rich had sent a screenshot of court availability for the following month.

In the shower, Dave assessed the damage. Blister on his right hand. Ache in his left shoulder. General soreness everywhere. Tomorrow he'd be properly sore. Tomorrow he'd struggle with stairs.

He couldn't wait.

That evening, after dinner (Sarah's elaborate vegetable situation turned out to be a curry, which was excellent), Dave found himself on YouTube again.

Just checking a few things.

Just seeing if there were any tips for beginners.

Just making sure he understood the basic grip technique properly.

By 10pm he'd watched eighteen videos and made notes on his phone under a new heading: "Improvement Plan - Week 1."

Sarah appeared in the doorway.

"Padel research again?"

Dave minimised YouTube quickly. "Maybe."

"You know you're allowed to enjoy things without imme-diately trying to optimise them?"

"I'm not trying to optimise it."

"You've made notes."

"Just a few thoughts about grip technique."

Sarah sat down next to him on the sofa. "I'm pleased you've found something you like."

"I don't like it. I'm terrible at it."

"You can be terrible at things and still like them."

"Can you though?"

"Dave. You spent six months learning to make bread during lockdown. Every single loaf was a disaster. The kitchen looked like a crime scene. You loved every minute of it."

This was fair.

"I just think," Dave said carefully, "that if I'm going to do something, I should try to do it properly."

"Right. Obviously." Sarah picked up the remote. "So this isn't going to become an obsession then?"

"Absolutely not."

"Good. Because you have form for this kind of thing."

"That's not true."

"You organised our bookshelves by colour."

"They look better that way."

"You can't find anything."

"Beauty requires sacrifice."

Sarah laughed, kissed his cheek. "Just... try to keep perspective, yeah? It's a game in a glass cage. It's not a life calling."

"I know that."

"Do you though?"

"Yes! It's just... fun. Exercise. Social. That's all."

"Okay." She didn't sound convinced.

Later, in bed, Dave lay awake thinking about Padel. About the weight of the paddle. About the angle of the ball coming off the glass. About positioning. About footwork. About Steve's easy competence and Rich's expensive kit and Mike's determination and the way the court had smelled like rubber and possibility.

His phone buzzed on the bedside table.

WhatsApp notification. Padel Lads .

Mike: "Just watched a tutorial on the bandeja shot. Game changer."

Dave picked up his phone, fully intending to just read the message and go to sleep.

Twenty minutes later he was deep into a YouTube rabbit hole about Spanish serving techniques.

Sarah, half-asleep beside him, muttered, "Turn the brightness down."

"Sorry."

"And go to sleep."

"Just one more video."

"Dave."

"It's about court positioning. It's important."

Sarah rolled over, pulling the duvet with her. "You're obsessed."

"I'm not obsessed."

"You're literally watching Padel videos at 11pm."

"That's just being prepared."

"That's obsession."

"It's research."

Sarah made a noise that suggested she knew she wasn't going to win this argument. "Just don't wake me up when you inevitably dream about it again."

"I'm not going to dream about it."

"You dreamed about it on Christmas night."

"That was different."

"How?"

"That was before I'd actually played. Now I have context."

Sarah didn't respond, which meant she was either asleep or had given up.

Dave watched three more videos, made extensive notes, and finally put his phone down at 11:47pm.

As he drifted off to sleep, his last thought was about whether changing his grip slightly might improve his serve accuracy.

He dreamed about Padel.

Obviously.

Chapter Three

The Second Session

Dave woke up on Sunday morning unable to move his arms properly.

"What's wrong with you?" Sarah asked, watching him attempt to reach for his phone on the bedside table like a T-Rex with motor function issues.

"Nothing. Just a bit stiff."

"A bit?"

"Fine. Very stiff. Extremely stiff. I may have permanently damaged myself."

"It's been less than twenty-four hours."

"I'm aware of that, thank you."

Sarah got out of bed with the kind of ease that suggested her body worked properly, unlike Dave's, which had apparently decided overnight to become one solid mass of pain.

"How bad is it?" she asked.

"On a scale of one to ten? Fourteen."

"Can you lift your arms above your head?"

Dave tried. His shoulders screamed in protest. He got them approximately to ear height before giving up.

"That's a no then."

"I'll be fine. Just need to move around a bit. Get the blood flowing."

Getting out of bed took three attempts and involved sounds Dave didn't know he could make. Showering required careful planning. Washing his hair meant accepting he couldn't quite reach the back of his head. Getting dressed was an exercise in humiliation - he put his t-shirt on backwards twice before Sarah took pity on him and helped.

"This is what happens," she said, pulling his t-shirt the right way round, "when forty-seven-year-old men who haven't exercised in a decade suddenly play sports."

"I exercise."

"Walking to the car doesn't count."

"What about the stairs at work?"

"Dave."

"Fine. Point taken."

Downstairs, Tom was eating cereal and scrolling through his phone. He looked up as Dave attempted to sit down, a process that involved lowering himself very slowly while holding the table for support.

"You alright, Dad?"

"Fine. Just played Padel yesterday."

"What's Padel?"

"Spanish tennis thing. In a cage."

Tom looked confused. "Why would you play tennis in a cage?"

"That's what makes it Padel."

"Right. Cool. You look like you've been hit by a car."

"Feel like it too."

By Monday morning, Dave had progressed from "completely immobile" to "mostly immobile." His colleagues noticed.

"You're walking funny," Priya from Accounts observed in the kitchen.

"Played sport on Saturday."

"What kind of sport makes you walk like that?"

"Padel."

"What's Padel?"

Dave was getting tired of explaining this. "It's like tennis but in a glass cage with different rules and a smaller court and you use a paddle instead of a racket."

Priya stared at him. "So... not like tennis then?"

"It's complicated."

"Right. Well. Hope you recover."

The WhatsApp group had been quiet on Sunday - everyone presumably suffering similar fates. But Monday morning brought renewed activity.

Mike, 8:47am: "Can anyone else not lift their arms?"

Steve, 8:51am: "I'm fine. You lot are just unfit."

Rich, 8:53am: "Had a sports massage yesterday. Highly recommend."

Mike, 8:54am: "Some of us can't just casually have sports massages, Richard."

Rich, 8:55am: "It's Rich."

Mike, 8:55am: "Richard feels more appropriate for someone with a massage therapist on speed dial."

Steve, 8:57am: "To be fair, I'm not fine. I'm lying. Everything hurts. I took four ibuprofen this morning."

Dave, 9:02am: "I couldn't wash the back of my head in the shower."

Rich, 9:03am: "That's normal soreness. Means the muscles are repairing. You'll be fine by Wednesday."

Mike, 9:04am: "We're playing Saturday though."

Rich, 9:04am: "Exactly. Perfect recovery time."

Steve, 9:06am: "Anyone actually got better at this yet or are we all still terrible?"

Dave had been thinking about this. He'd been thinking about it a lot. In fact, he'd spent most of Sunday evening on YouTube despite his arms barely functioning, watching tutorial after tutorial.

Dave, 9:15am: "I've been researching grip techniques. I think we might be holding the paddles wrong."

Mike, 9:16am: "We're definitely holding them wrong. I watched a video. Continental grip vs Eastern grip. Very technical."

Steve, 9:18am: "You two have already fallen down the YouTube rabbit hole haven't you?"

Dave, 9:18am: "What? No. Just doing a bit of research."

Rich, 9:19am: "Dave mate, how many videos have you watched?"

Dave, 9:22am: "A reasonable amount."

Mike, 9:22am: "He's watched loads. I can tell."

Dave, 9:23am: "Maybe thirty."

Steve, 9:23am: "THIRTY?!"

Dave, 9:24am: "Could be forty. I wasn't counting."

Rich, 9:25am: "We played ONE session."

Dave, 9:26am: "And I was terrible. I need to understand the fundamentals."

Mike, 9:27am: "I've only watched fifteen."

Steve, 9:28am: "Only fifteen? Christ, you're both mental."

Rich, 9:29am: "This is good though. Shows commitment. I like it."

The week crawled by with painful slowness. Dave's arms slowly remembered how to function properly. By Tuesday he could wash his hair. By Wednesday he could put on his coat without assistance. By Thursday he almost felt normal.

He'd also watched another twenty-three videos.

Sarah had noticed.

"You're on YouTube again," she observed on Wednesday evening.

"Just background noise while I cook."

"You're not cooking. I'm cooking. You're watching a Spanish man explain serve techniques."

"He makes good points."

"Dave."

"What?"

"You're doing the thing."

"What thing?"

"The obsession thing. The thing where you find something new and suddenly it's all you think about."

"That's not true."

"You've got a spreadsheet."

"How do you know about the spreadsheet?"

"Because I know you. Of course you've got a spreadsheet. What's it tracking?"

Dave considered lying. "Points scored. Successful serves. Return percentage. Areas for improvement."

"You've played once."

"Which means I have baseline data."

Sarah put down the wooden spoon she'd been using to stir pasta. "Dave. I love you. You know I love you. But you need to relax about this."

"I am relaxed."

"You're the opposite of relaxed. You're wound tighter than... than..." She struggled for a comparison.

"A tennis racket?" Dave offered.

"It's not tennis!"

"That's what I keep saying!"

They stared at each other. Sarah's mouth twitched.

"You're impossible," she said, but she was smiling.

"I just want to not be terrible at it."

"You've played once. Everyone's terrible at first."

"Rich isn't terrible."

"Rich has probably been playing for years."

"Six months apparently."

"Well then. You've got six months to catch up."

Dave knew she was right. He knew he was being ridiculous. He also knew he was going to carry on watching YouTube videos and updating his spreadsheet and thinking about grip techniques while trying to fall asleep.

By Friday evening, the WhatsApp group was buzzing with nervous energy.

Steve, 6:34pm: "Everyone ready for tomorrow?"

Rich, 6:41pm: "Got a new paddle arriving today actually. Want to test it out."

Mike, 6:43pm: "You bought a new paddle? You've got a paddle!"

Rich, 6:44pm: "That's my old one. This one's got a different sweet spot. Should improve my control."

Dave, 6:47pm: "How many paddles do you have?"

Rich, 6:48pm: "Three now. Different conditions require different equipment."

Steve, 6:49pm: "It's an indoor court. The conditions are identical every week."

Rich, 6:50pm: "Court temperature varies. Humidity affects ball bounce."

Mike, 6:51pm: "Are you actually serious?"

Rich, 6:52pm: "Professional players have multiple paddles. I'm just following best practice."

Dave found himself Googling paddle specifications. There were, he discovered, hundreds of options. Different materials. Different weights. Different balance points. Different shapes affecting power versus control.

He created a new tab in his spreadsheet: "Equipment Research."

Sarah walked past, saw the screen, sighed deeply, and kept walking.

Saturday morning arrived with the kind of nervous energy Dave hadn't felt since... actually, he couldn't remember the last time he'd felt nervous about anything recreational. Work presentations, sure. Difficult conversations, absolutely. But sport? Not since he was a teenager.

"You're up early," Sarah observed at 7am.

"Couldn't sleep."

"Because of Padel?"

"No. Well. Maybe. Bit."

"Dave, it's a game."

"I know that."

"Then why are you stressed?"

"I'm not stressed."

"You're doing that thing with your jaw."

Dave consciously relaxed his jaw, which he hadn't realised was clenched. "I just want to do better than last week."

"You scored two points. Literally any improvement is better."

"Exactly. Lot of pressure."

Sarah kissed his forehead. "Try to have fun, yeah? That's the actual point."

Dave drove to ActiveLife with his gym bag (he'd bought a proper gym bag, the carrier bag from last week had seemed unprofessional) and a sense of determination that was probably disproportionate to the activity at hand.

The others were already there. Rich had brought his new paddle - sleek, black, with "HEAD" written in silver letters. It looked, Dave thought, like it cost more than his weekly food shop.

"Nice paddle," Dave said.

"Carbon fibre face. EVA foam core. Optimises power and control." Rich said this like it was completely normal to know the internal composition of sporting equipment.

Steve was using the same paddle as last week. So was Mike. So was Dave.

They were absolutely fine with their paddles.

Definitely not feeling inadequate about their paddles.

Not at all.

The session started. Dave served first.

The ball hit the net.

"Shake it off," Rich called. "Just nerves."

Dave served again. This time the ball went long.

"Bit less power," Mike suggested.

Third serve. Finally, it went over. Steve returned it gently. Dave positioned himself, remembered everything he'd learned about grip technique and footwork and court positioning, swung carefully—

And hit a perfect return straight down the middle.

Steve returned it. Mike hit it back. Rich returned again. Dave hit it once more—

The rally continued. Five shots. Six. Seven.

On the eighth shot, Mike hit it into the net.

They'd lost the point, but nobody cared. They'd had an actual rally. An actual, genuine, multi-shot rally.

"Did that just happen?" Mike asked.

"That just happened," Steve confirmed.

"We did a rally!"

"Mate, calm down," Rich said, but he was grinning. "Let's see if you can do it again."

They could. Not every time. But sometimes. Occasionally they'd string together ten shots. Once they managed fifteen before Steve hit it wide.

They still lost the first game 11-3, but those three points felt earned rather than pitied.

"You two have improved," Rich said during the water break.

"Really?" Dave tried not to sound too eager.

"Yeah, definitely. Your positioning's better. You're actually moving your feet now instead of just reaching."

"I watched some videos," Dave admitted.

"Me too," Mike added.

Steve laughed. "How many?"

"A few."

"How many's a few?"

Dave and Mike looked at each other.

"Maybe sixty," Dave said.

"Combined?" Steve asked hopefully.

"Each."

"Bloody hell. You two are committed, I'll give you that."

Rich nodded approvingly. "That's what it takes though. Theory and practice. Can't just rock up and expect to improve."

They played two more games. Lost them both, but by smaller margins. 11-6. Then 11-7.

"Nearly into double figures," Mike said. "We're basically professionals now."

"Steady on," Steve said. "You still hit yourself in the face with the paddle."

"Only once this week! That's a fifty percent improvement!"

After the session, in the changing rooms, Rich brought up an idea that had clearly been brewing.

"So," he said, "I've been thinking. We're doing this every week anyway. What if we made it more official?"

"Official how?" Dave asked.

"Well, ActiveLife runs leagues. Beginners' league starts in April. We could enter. As a team."

There was a pause.

"A league?" Mike said. "Like, competitive?"

"Not serious competitive. Just... you know, league competitive. Matches. Points. Standings."

"That's definitely serious competitive," Steve said.

"It's just for fun."

"Leagues are never just for fun," Dave said. "Leagues have winners and losers. Leagues have rankings. Leagues are definitionally not just for fun."

"Exactly," Rich said. "So what do you think?"

Dave looked at Mike. Mike looked at Steve. Steve looked at Rich.

"I'm in," Steve said.

"Yeah, why not," Mike added.

They all looked at Dave.

The sensible part of Dave's brain pointed out that he'd played Padel twice. That he was terrible at it. That entering a league after two sessions was ridiculous. That he had a full-time job and family commitments and absolutely no business adding competitive sports to his schedule.

"I'm in," Dave said.

"Excellent!" Rich pulled out his phone. "I'll register us. We need a team name."

"The Padel Lads?" Mike suggested.

"Too obvious."

"The Glass Ceiling?" Dave tried.

"Makes no sense."

"The Net Losers?" Steve offered.

"Bit negative."

They threw out suggestions. Most were terrible. Some were unprintable. Eventually they settled on "The Rookies" which at least had the benefit of being accurate.

Rich completed the registration on his phone. "Done. We're in. First match is mid-April. Gives us about ten weeks to not be completely embarrassing."

"Ten weeks," Dave repeated. "That's plenty of time."

"To go from terrible to mediocre?" Steve said. "Maybe."

"Challenge accepted," Mike said.

In the car park, saying their goodbyes, making plans for next week, Dave felt something he hadn't felt in years. Purpose, maybe. Or just anticipation. The sense that Saturday mornings now meant something.

Rich drove off in his Porsche Cayenne. Steve drove off in his ancient Vauxhall Corsa. Mike waved from his sensible Volvo estate.

Dave sat in his Škoda for a moment before starting the engine.

They were entering a league. An actual league. They were going to play matches against other teams. There would be scores. And rankings. And possibly humiliation.

Dave opened his phone and created a new note: "League Preparation - Week 1."

His phone buzzed. WhatsApp.

Mike: "Did we just commit to a league?"

Steve: "We did."

Rich: "Ten weeks to get good. Plenty of time."

Dave: "We're going to need more practice."

Mike: "Agreed. What about Wednesday evenings?"

Rich: "I can do Wednesdays."

Steve: "Wednesdays work."

Dave: "Booking now."

He opened the ActiveLife app. There was one slot available for Wednesday at 7pm. He booked it immediately.

Then he opened YouTube.

Just to check a few things.

Just to see if there were any league-specific strategies he should know about.

Just to make sure he understood advanced serving techniques.

By the time he got home, he'd watched eleven videos and made extensive notes.

Sarah was in the garden, reading.

"How was it?" she called.

"Good! We're entering a league!"

Sarah looked up from her book. "A league?"

"Beginners' league. Starts in April."

"Right. That's... quite committed for someone who's played twice."

"Three times if you count Wednesday."

"You're playing Wednesday?"

"Need more practice before the league starts."

Sarah marked her page and closed the book. "Dave. You said this wasn't going to become an obsession."

"It's not an obsession. It's just preparation."

"You're playing twice a week."

"That's very reasonable actually. Rich plays four times a week."

"Rich is clearly mental."

"Rich is committed to excellence."

"Rich needs a hobby."

"Rich has a hobby. Padel."

Sarah stood up. "Dave. I'm saying this with love. You're doing the thing again."

"What thing?"

"The spreadsheet thing. The YouTube thing. The completely-losing-perspective thing."

"I have perfect perspective."

"Do you though?"

"Yes! I'm just... interested. That's all. Interested in being less terrible at something I've started doing. That's normal. That's healthy."

Sarah studied him for a moment. "Okay. But when you start waking up at midnight to book courts, I'm staging an intervention."

"That's not going to happen."

"Right."

"It's not!"

"If you say so."

That evening, Dave set an alarm for 11:58pm. Just in case he needed to book next week's Saturday slot at midnight.

Just to be safe.

Just to be prepared.

When it went off, Sarah rolled over. "Are you actually serious?"

"It's just this once."

"It's never just once with you."

Dave booked the court. And the Wednesday after. And the Saturday after that.

"Done," he said, silencing his phone.

"You're ridiculous," Sarah muttered.

"I know."

"This is ridiculous."

"I know."

"You're going to be insufferable about this, aren't you?"

Dave thought about it. "Probably."

Sarah was quiet for a moment. Then: "Just promise me you'll still be fun at parties."

"When am I ever fun at parties?"

"Fair point. Promise me you won't bore everyone talking about Padel then."

"I promise."

This was a lie. Dave knew it was a lie. Sarah knew it was a lie.

But they both pretended it wasn't, because that's what you do when you love someone who's just discovered a new obsession.

Dave lay in the dark, thinking about leagues and grip techniques and court positioning and Wednesday evening sessions.

Just thinking.

Not obsessing.

Definitely not obsessing.

His phone buzzed. WhatsApp.

Rich: "Anyone else researching league tactics?"

Mike: "Obviously."

Steve: "Obviously not."

Dave: "Might have looked into it a bit."

Rich: "We should probably practice more than twice a week."

Steve: "How much more?"

Rich: "Four times would be ideal."

Mike: "Four times a week? Are you mental?"

Rich: "Rafael Nadal trained six days a week."

Dave: "We're not Rafael Nadal."

Rich: "Not with that attitude."

Steve: "I've got work. And a life."

Rich: "So? We all have work."

Mike: "Rich mate, some of us can't just take Tuesday mornings off for Padel."

Rich: "Fair point. What about weekends? Saturday and Sunday?"

There was a pause in the chat. Dave could practically hear everyone considering it.

Mike: "Sarah would kill me if I played both days."

Dave: "Same."

Steve: "I mean... I could probably do both days."

Rich: "That's the spirit."

Dave stared at the screen. Two days a week was already pushing it. Two weekend days would be insane.

Dave: "Maybe we could do Sunday mornings occasionally? Like, once a month?"

Mike: "Once a month is acceptable."

Rich: "Once a month is barely training."

Steve: "It's training plus recreation. Best of both worlds."

Rich: "Fine. But we're taking this seriously, right? The league?"

Dave looked at the ceiling. At Sarah sleeping beside him. At the sensible, reasonable life he'd built.

Dave: "Absolutely. Taking it very seriously."

Mike: "Definitely."

Steve: "100%."

Rich: "Good. Right. See you Wednesday. 7pm sharp."

Dave put his phone on the bedside table. Face down. Screen off.

Picked it up again thirty seconds later.

Opened YouTube.

Just one more video.

Just to be sure he understood the bandeja shot properly.

Just to be prepared for Wednesday.

By the time he fell asleep at 1:47am, he'd watched nine more videos and created a new spreadsheet tab titled "League Strategy."

He dreamed about the league trophy.

They hadn't won it yet.

They probably wouldn't win it.

But in his dream, they absolutely did.

Chapter Four
The Equipment Spiral

Three weeks into their Padel journey, Dave made a discovery that would prove financially dangerous: there were entire websites dedicated to Padel equipment.

Not just one or two items. Hundreds. Thousands, possibly. Paddles in every conceivable shape, size, and price point. Shoes specifically designed for Padel courts. Bags with special compartments for paddles. Grips. Overgrips. Wristbands. Headbands. Clothes with moisture-wicking properties Dave didn't know existed.

It was 11:34pm on a Tuesday. Dave should have been asleep. Instead, he was scrolling through "PadelPro UK" with the intensity of someone conducting vital research.

"What are you doing?" Sarah asked, not opening her eyes.

"Just looking at something."

"Padel something?"

"Might be."

"Dave."

"I'm just browsing. There's no harm in browsing."

"That's what you said before you bought seventeen different types of coffee beans."

"That was different. That was an investment in morning productivity."

"We're still working through them. There's a bag from 2023 in the cupboard."

Dave put his phone down. Picked it up again. Put it down.

"The thing is," he said, "I think our equipment might be holding us back."

Sarah opened one eye. "You've been playing for three weeks."

"Exactly. Time to upgrade."

"Upgrade from what? The rental paddles you've been using?"

"We have been using rentals. Which is fine for beginners. But we're not really beginners anymore, are we? We've played... let me check..." Dave opened his spreadsheet. "Fourteen sessions."

"Fourteen sessions in three weeks?"

"We've been doing extra practice."

"How much extra practice?"

"Just a bit. Anyway, the point is, rental paddles are generic. They're one-size-fits-all. They don't account for individual playing style or skill level."

"You don't have a playing style yet. You just hit the ball and hope."

This was unfortunately accurate, but Dave pressed on anyway.

"The thing is, if you look at the research—"

"There's research?"

"YouTube videos. Very informative. Different paddle shapes affect your game. Round is for control, diamond is for power, teardrop is balanced. I need to figure out which one suits me."

"How do you figure that out?"

"Well, ideally you'd try all three types, assess your natural playing tendency, and make an informed decision based on—"

"Dave."

"What?"

"Just buy a paddle. Any paddle. They're all fine."

"They're really not all fine, Sarah. There's carbon fiber faces versus fiberglass, EVA foam versus FOAM rubber cores, rough surfaces versus smooth, and don't even get me started on balance points—"

Sarah put her pillow over her face and made a muffled sound that Dave interpreted as either supportive encouragement or the opposite of that.

The WhatsApp group had been having similar conversations.

Mike, 9:47am: "So. Paddles. Are we buying our own?"

Rich, 9:52am: "Obviously. Can't compete with rental equipment."

Steve, 9:54am: "The rentals are fine."

Rich, 9:55am: "The rentals are terrible. No feel. Wrong grip size. Poor weight distribution."

Mike, 9:57am: "How much do decent paddles cost?"

Rich, 9:58am: "Depends what you mean by decent."

Steve, 10:02am: "Under £50?"

Rich, 10:03am: "That's not decent. That's barely functional."

Mike, 10:04am: "What would you recommend then?"

Rich, 10:05am: "For beginners? Nothing under £150. Ideally £200+."

Steve, 10:06am: "£200?! For a paddle?!"

Rich, 10:07am: "You get what you pay for."

Dave, 10:15am: "I've been researching. There's a good middle ground around £100-120. Respectable brands. Decent materials."

Mike, 10:16am: "That's still quite a lot for something we might not stick with."

Rich, 10:17am: "We're in a league. We're sticking with it."

Steve, 10:19am: "Some of us have budgets."

There was a pause in the chat. Dave could practically feel the awkwardness through the screen.

Rich, 10:22am: "Right. Yeah. Sorry. What's everyone's budget?"

Mike, 10:23am: "£100 max."

Dave, 10:24am: "Same."

Steve, 10:26am: "I was thinking more like £50."

Rich, 10:27am: "Right. Okay. That's... challenging. But doable."

Dave spent his lunch break researching paddles in the £100 range. There were, he discovered, at least forty viable options. All claiming to be perfect for intermediate players. All with slightly different specifications that supposedly affected performance in ways Dave couldn't quite understand but felt he should.

By 2pm he'd created a new spreadsheet: "Paddle Comparison Matrix."

By 3pm he'd added seventeen different models with detailed specs.

By 4pm Priya from Accounts found him in the kitchen staring at his phone with an intensity that suggested either a family emergency or sporting equipment research.

"You alright?" she asked.

"Trying to decide between EVA foam and FOAM rubber cores."

"Right. For...?"

"Padel paddle."

"The cage tennis thing?"

"It's not tennis."

"Right. Sorry. The cage not-tennis thing."

"Exactly."

Priya made her coffee in silence, clearly deciding this wasn't a conversation she wanted to continue.

That evening, Dave presented his research to Sarah over dinner.

"So," he said, pulling up his spreadsheet on his phone, "I've narrowed it down to five options."

"Great. Pick one."

"It's not that simple. Look." He turned the phone to show her. "This one has a carbon fiber face which gives better power, but this one has a textured surface for more spin. This one's round which means control, but this one's teardrop which means balance. This one—"

"Dave. They're all fine. Just pick one."

"But what if I pick wrong?"

"Then you'll have learned something and you can buy another one."

"I can't just buy another one. They're £100 each!"

"Then get it right the first time."

"That's what I'm trying to do!"

Sarah put down her fork. "Dave. Listen to me. You are overthinking this. They are all adequate paddles that will serve your current needs, which is to hit a ball in a glass cage with your mates on weekends. You do not need the optimal paddle. You need a paddle. Any paddle. Pick one by tomorrow or I'm picking one for you."

Dave looked at his spreadsheet. At the hours of research. At the carefully compiled specifications and user reviews and professional assessments.

"Fine," he said. "I'll decide tonight."

He decided at 11:47pm after watching six more comparison videos and reading forty-three customer reviews.

The Bullpadel Vertex. £119.99. Carbon fiber face. EVA foam core. Teardrop shape. 365g weight. "Perfect for intermediate players looking to develop their all-round game."

He added it to his basket. Hovered over checkout.

This was a lot of money for something he'd only been doing for three weeks.

He clicked checkout.

The confirmation email arrived thirty seconds later. Dave felt a rush of something - excitement mixed with guilt mixed with anticipation.

He'd bought his own paddle.

He was officially committed now.

The WhatsApp group exploded the next morning when Dave shared his purchase.

Dave, 8:34am: "Just ordered a Bullpadel Vertex."

Mike, 8:36am: "You actually did it?"

Dave, 8:37am: "Seemed like time."

Rich, 8:38am: "Good choice. Solid intermediate paddle."

Steve, 8:41am: "How much?"

Dave, 8:42am: "£120."

Steve, 8:43am: "Bloody hell."

Mike, 8:45am: "I've been looking at the Adidas Adipower. Anyone used one?"

Rich, 8:46am: "Decent. Bit heavy for beginners though."

Mike, 8:47am: "We're not beginners anymore. We've played fourteen sessions."

Dave, 8:48am: "That's what I said!"

Steve, 8:51am: "I'm still using the rental."

Rich, 8:52am: "Steve mate, you need your own equipment."

Steve, 8:54am: "The rental works fine."

Rich, 8:55am: "It's holding you back."

Steve, 8:57am: "Or I'm just not very good."

Mike, 8:58am: "Steve, you're better than me and Dave combined."

Dave, 8:59am: "Speak for yourself."

Mike, 8:59am: "You hit yourself in the face with your paddle yesterday."

Dave, 9:00am: "That was a freak accident."

Rich, 9:02am: "Steve, seriously though. Own paddle makes a difference. I'll help you find something in budget."

Steve, 9:05am: "Thanks but I'm fine."

Dave could tell Steve wasn't fine. Could tell there was something else going on. But the group chat wasn't the place to push it.

The paddle arrived two days later. Dave had, embarrassingly, tracked the delivery obsessively. Checked the tracking number seventeen times. Been home by 4:30pm to ensure he didn't miss it.

Sarah watched him open the box like it contained the Holy Grail.

"It's a paddle," she said.

"It's not just a paddle. It's a Bullpadel Vertex. Carbon fiber face. Look at the surface texture." He ran his finger across it reverently.

"Looks like a paddle to me."

"You can't appreciate the craftsmanship."

"You're right. I can't. Because it's a paddle."

Dave ignored her. He weighed it in his hand. Tested the grip. Did a few practice swings in the living room.

"Dave. Stop swinging that in the house."

"I'm just getting a feel for it."

"Get a feel for it in the cage where you can't break anything."

Saturday morning couldn't come fast enough. Dave arrived at ActiveLife twenty minutes early, paddle in its new protective case (purchased separately for £24.99, also carbon fiber).

Rich was already there, also with his paddle. They caught each other's eye and shared a nod of mutual understanding. Mike arrived ten minutes later with a box under his arm.

"You bought one!" Dave said.

"Adidas Adipower. Just arrived. Haven't even taken it out the box yet."

They gathered at their court like kids on Christmas morning, comparing purchases with an enthusiasm that would have been endearing if it weren't so ridiculous.

Rich nodded approvingly at Dave's choice. "Good paddle. Should suit your game."

"What is my game?" Dave asked.

"Don't know yet. But when you develop one, this'll suit it."

Mike's Adipower was heavier than expected. He did a few practice swings and nearly hit Steve, who'd arrived with his usual rental paddle.

"You didn't buy one?" Mike asked.

"Still thinking about it," Steve said, in a tone that suggested he wasn't thinking about it at all.

They started playing. Dave served with his new paddle. It felt different. Better, he thought, though he couldn't quite articulate how. The ball went exactly where it had gone with the rental paddle, which is to say, not quite where he'd aimed.

But it felt more intentional somehow.

Mike was having similar feelings about his purchase. "It's definitely better," he declared after his second serve went into the net.

"How can you tell?" Steve asked.

"Just... the feel. The response. The..." Mike struggled for technical language. "The paddleness of it."

"That's not a word."

"It should be."

They played three games. Lost all three, but Dave felt there was something different about the quality of their losing. More technical. More informed.

"We're getting better," he said during the break.

"We're really not," Steve said. "We're just spending more money."

"Equipment matters though," Rich said, opening what Dave now recognised as a very expensive water bottle. "Professional tools for professional play."

"We're not professionals."

"Not yet. But we're in a league. That's semi-professional."

"That's absolutely not what semi-professional means," Mike said.

After the session, in the changing rooms, Rich pulled Steve aside. Dave and Mike pretended not to eavesdrop while absolutely eavesdropping.

"Steve, mate," Rich said quietly. "About the paddle thing."

"I'm fine with the rental."

"I know you are. But listen. I've got a spare. My second one. The Head Evo. It's just sitting at home. You'd be doing me a favour taking it off my hands."

"Rich—"

"I'm serious. I'm never going to use it. Wrong balance for my play style. You'd actually be helping me out."

There was a pause.

"I can't just take your paddle," Steve said.

"You're not taking it. I'm lending it. Indefinitely. Try it. If you don't like it, give it back."

Another pause.

"How much did it cost?" Steve asked.

"Doesn't matter."

"Rich."

"About £180. But that's not—"

"I can't accept a £180 paddle."

"Steve. Listen. I bought it. Didn't like it. It's been in my cupboard for three months. You using it gives it purpose. Otherwise it's just wasted money. You'd literally be doing me a favour."

Dave watched Steve's face. Saw him wrestling with pride and practicality.

"Just try it," Rich said. "One session. If you hate it, give it back. No pressure."

"Fine," Steve said eventually. "One session. But I'm paying you something for it."

"Absolutely not."

"Rich—"

"Steve. Mate. We're a team, yeah? Teams help each other out. That's what this is. Team support."

Steve looked like he wanted to argue but couldn't quite find the words.

"I'll bring it Wednesday," Rich said, as if the matter was settled.

In the car park, Dave and Mike had their own debrief.

"That was decent of Rich," Mike said.

"Yeah. Good lad."

"Makes you wonder though."

"What?"

"How much money does he actually have? Like, casually giving away £180 paddles."

Dave had been wondering the same thing. "Something in property development, he said."

"That's not a real answer though, is it? That's what people say when they're rich but don't want to explain how."

"Maybe he's just successful."

"Maybe he's a drug dealer."

"He's not a drug dealer."

"How do you know?"

"Drug dealers don't wear Head-to-Toe-Adidas and say things like 'optimal sweet spot.'"

"Fair point."

They stood in the February cold, steam rising from their cooling bodies, talking about Rich's mysterious wealth like it was the most fascinating topic in the world.

"We should probably go home," Dave said eventually.

"Probably."

Neither of them moved.

"New paddles are good though," Mike said.

"Definitely make a difference."

"The weight distribution is better."

"And the grip."

"Exactly."

They stood there a moment longer.

"Sarah's going to kill me when she sees the credit card bill," Dave said.

"Clare already knows. She says I'm having a midlife crisis."

"Are we having midlife crises?"

"Mate, we're forty-seven and we just spent £250 on paddles for a sport we've done for three weeks. We're definitely having midlife crises."

"At least we're doing it together."

"That's the spirit."

Dave drove home with his paddle in its protective case on the passenger seat, occasionally glancing at it like it might disappear if he looked away.

Sarah was in the kitchen when he got home.

"How was it?"

"Good! The new paddle definitely makes a difference."

"Does it?"

"Absolutely. The ball response is clearer. The sweet spot is larger. The—"

"Dave. Did you win?"

"Well, no. But that's not the point."

"What is the point?"

"The point is progression. Development. Technical improvement."

"So you lost."

"We lost with better technique."

Sarah smiled despite herself. "You're ridiculous."

"I know."

"This is costing us money."

"It's an investment in health."

"It's an investment in being less terrible at a sport you're still terrible at."

"Same thing."

That evening, Dave cleaned his paddle with a special cleaning solution (£8.99, specifically formulated for carbon fiber faces). He watched a YouTube video about paddle maintenance. He learned there were optimal storage temperatures. That you shouldn't leave it in the car. That direct sunlight could damage the core.

He created a new note on his phone: "Paddle Care Instructions."

At 10:34pm, the WhatsApp group buzzed.

Rich: "Remembered to clean your paddles?"

Dave: "Just finished."

Mike: "Should I be cleaning it?"

Rich: "Absolutely. Carbon fiber needs proper maintenance."

Steve: "It's been three hours."

Rich: "Sweat is corrosive."

Mike: "Is it?"

Dave: "I'll send you a video."

Steve: "Please don't send me a video."

Dave: "Sent."

Steve: "I hate you all."

Mike: "This is a thirteen-minute video about paddle cleaning."

Dave: "It's very thorough."

Rich: "Actually quite informative."

Steve: "You're all mental."

But Dave noticed Steve's "read" receipt at 10:47pm. And again at 11:03pm.

He'd watched the video.

They all had.

Because that's what you did when you'd spent £120 on a paddle.

You watched the thirteen-minute maintenance video.

Obviously.

Dave lay in bed that night thinking about his paddle downstairs in its case, stored at optimal temperature away from direct sunlight.

"You're thinking about your paddle, aren't you?" Sarah said in the dark.

"No."

"You are."

"Maybe."

"Dave."

"It was expensive. I want to look after it properly."

"It's a paddle. Not a child."

"It's a carbon fiber paddle with an EVA foam core."

"That means nothing to me."

"I know. But it means something to me."

Sarah rolled over. "Just promise me this is it. No more purchases."

"This is it. Absolutely. Just the paddle."

"Promise?"

"Promise."

This was, of course, a lie.

Within a week Dave would discover that proper Padel shoes existed.

Within two weeks he'd order special grip tape.

Within three weeks he'd buy a paddle bag with temperature-controlled compartment.

But for now, in this moment, Dave genuinely believed he was done spending money on Padel equipment.

Sarah knew better.

She'd seen this pattern before.

But she loved him anyway.

Even if he was absolutely, demonstrably, having a midlife crisis in a glass cage with three other middle-aged men.

Especially because of that, maybe.

Chapter Five
The Lesson

It was Mike who first suggested they get professional coaching.

Mike, 10:23am: "So. Random thought. Should we get lessons?"

Rich, 10:27am: "Absolutely. Been thinking the same thing."

Dave, 10:31am: "We've been playing for six weeks. Isn't that a bit soon?"

Rich, 10:32am: "It's never too soon for proper technique. Bad habits form early."

Steve, 10:34am: "How much do lessons cost?"

Rich, 10:35am: "Group sessions are about £60 for an hour. Split four ways, that's £15 each."

Mike, 10:37am: "That's actually reasonable."

Steve, 10:38am: "That's more than I spend on food some days."

There was a pause in the chat.

Rich, 10:41am: "Steve mate, it's an investment."

Steve, 10:42am: "In what?"

Rich, 10:43am: "In not being shit."

Dave, 10:45am: "When you put it like that..."

Mike, 10:46am: "I'm in. We need help. Yesterday I served and the ball went backwards."

Dave, 10:47am: "How did you manage that?"

Mike, 10:48am: "No idea. That's why we need lessons."

Rich, 10:50am: "Right. I'll book something. There's a Spanish coach at ActiveLife. Carlos. Supposed to be excellent."

Steve, 10:52am: "How do you know he's excellent?"

Rich, 10:53am: "Reviews on the website. 4.9 stars."

Dave, 10:54am: "What kind of psychopath gives a Padel coach less than 5 stars?"

Mike, 10:55am: "Someone who still can't serve probably."

The lesson was booked for the following Wednesday evening. Dave spent the intervening days watching YouTube videos about "how to prepare for Padel coaching" which turned out to be a real thing that real people had made content about.

Sarah caught him making notes on his phone.

"What are you doing?"

"Preparing questions for the coach."

"Dave. You're paying him to teach you. Not interview him."

"But I want to make the most of the session. £15 is a lot of money."

"It's £15."

"Exactly. That's... three coffees."

"That's not how money works."

"It's how my brain works."

By Wednesday evening, Dave had a list of seventeen questions ranging from "optimal serving technique" to "psychological approaches to competitive play."

They arrived at Court 3 at 6:55pm. Carlos was already there, doing stretches that suggested his body worked in ways theirs definitely didn't.

He was probably mid-forties, lean, wearing proper Padel gear - shorts that weren't too long or too short, a fitted technical shirt, shoes that looked like they'd been de-signed by NASA. His skin had the kind of tan that came from actual sunshine rather than British summers.

"Gentlemen!" he said, accent definitely Spanish but softened by years in the UK. "You are my six o'clock group, yes?"

"That's us," Rich said. "Thanks for fitting us in."

"No problem. Always happy to help new players." Carlos looked them over with an expression that was probably meant to be encouraging but came across as mildly concerned. "So. You have been playing how long?"

"Six weeks," Dave said.

"Seven," Mike corrected.

"Six and a half," Rich compromised.

Carlos nodded. "Okay. Good. That is... good. Not too many bad habits yet. Probably. So, tell me. What do you want to work on?"

They all spoke at once.

"Serving—"

"Positioning—"

"Return technique—"

"Everything—"

Carlos held up his hand. "Okay, okay. I understand. Everything. We start with basics then. Show me how you serve."

Dave went first. He positioned himself carefully, bounced the ball once, twice, three times. Took a breath. Served.

The ball hit the net.

"Okay," Carlos said, in a tone that suggested he'd seen this before. "Try again."

Dave served again. This time it went over but with all the power and accuracy of a deflating balloon.

Carlos watched Mike serve (into the side wall), Rich serve (competently), and Steve serve (surprisingly well, even with the rental paddle).

"Right," Carlos said. "I see the problems. Many problems. We fix them. But first..." He walked to the baseline. "Watch."

He served. The ball moved with purpose. Bounced precisely in the service box. Hit the back glass at an angle that made it basically unreturnable.

"This," Carlos said, "is how you serve. Now. Let me show you what you are doing."

What followed was possibly the most humbling hour of Dave's adult life.

Carlos demonstrated their serves. All of them. With cruel accuracy. He mimicked Dave's overthinking pause. Mike's panicked flail. Even Rich's slightly-too-careful technique.

"You are all," Carlos said, not unkindly, "thinking too much. Padel is not chess. Is not mathematics. Is muscle memory and feeling."

"But surely," Dave said, "understanding the theory helps?"

"Theory is good. But you—" Carlos pointed at Dave's head "—too much thinking. Not enough doing."

"I've watched a lot of videos."

"I can tell. You serve like someone who has watched videos. Not like someone who has served."

This felt deeply unfair but was also completely accurate.

Carlos worked through their serves individually. Adjusted their grips. Changed their stance. Modified their follow-through. Each time, the difference was noticeable. Not dramatic - they weren't suddenly serving like professionals - but better. Cleaner. More controlled.

"Again," Carlos said, for the forty-seventh time.

Dave served. The ball went exactly where he'd aimed. For the first time in seven weeks, he'd served with intention and accuracy.

"Yes!" Carlos clapped. "This! This is serving! Remember this feeling!"

Dave tried to remember. Tried to capture exactly what he'd done. Tried to—

"Stop thinking!" Carlos said. "Just feel it! Do it again!"

Dave did it again. Hit the net.

"You thought about it," Carlos said. "Don't think. Just serve."

"How can I not think about serving while I'm serving?"

"This is your problem. Too much brain. Not enough..." Carlos gestured vaguely at his own body. "...body knowing."

They moved on to returns. Then positioning. Then the mysterious bandeja shot that Dave had been trying to understand via YouTube for six weeks.

Carlos demonstrated. The shot was somehow both aggressive and controlled, sending the ball bouncing away from the opponents with spin that looked physically impossible.

"This," he said, "is not for beginners."

"We're not beginners," Rich protested. "We've been playing seven weeks."

Carlos looked at him. Said nothing. The silence communicated everything.

"Okay," Rich admitted. "We're beginners."

"You are..." Carlos searched for a diplomatic word. "...developing players."

"That's worse," Steve muttered.

They practiced the bandeja anyway. Or tried to. Mike hit himself in the face with his paddle. Dave shanked the ball into the wire mesh. Rich actually made reasonable contact but sent it flying out of the court entirely. Steve's rental paddle made a concerning cracking sound.

"This will take time," Carlos said, with the patience of a man who'd clearly seen worse. "Is okay. You practice. You improve. Maybe in six months—"

"Six months?" Dave said.

"Maybe six months you can do bandeja in game situation. For now, just try not to hit yourself."

"That's a low bar," Mike said.

"Is appropriate bar for your level."

After an hour, they were all sweating, exhausted, and significantly more aware of how little they actually knew about Padel.

Carlos gathered them at the net for a final debrief.

"You have potential," he said, which Dave suspected was something he said to everyone who paid him. "But you must practice correctly. Not just play. Practice the things I showed you. Slow repetition. Muscle memory."

"Should we book another lesson?" Rich asked.

"Maybe in three weeks. Give you time to practice. Otherwise you just pay me to tell you same things again."

This seemed honest enough that Dave believed him.

"One more thing," Carlos said. "You are entering league, yes?"

"How did you know?" Mike asked.

"I see your names on registration. Is good. But..." He paused, clearly choosing his words carefully. "League is competitive. Other teams have been playing long time. You should manage expectations."

"We're going to get destroyed, aren't we?" Steve said.

Carlos smiled. "Destroyed is strong word. Maybe just... very much defeated."

"Great. Looking forward to it."

"But is okay! Is how you learn! You play better teams, you improve faster. Just... maybe prepare for losing."

"We're already very good at losing," Dave said.

"Then you are prepared!"

They paid Carlos, thanked him profusely, and trudged to the changing rooms with the slightly dazed expression of people who'd just been professionally told they were terrible at something.

"That was humbling," Mike said.

"That was humiliating," Dave corrected.

"Educational humiliation," Rich suggested.

"Is that a thing?"

"It is now."

Steve was quiet, stuffing his rental paddle back in his bag with more force than necessary.

"You alright?" Dave asked.

"Fine. Just... that was a lot."

"He was pretty direct."

"Not about that. Just... you heard what he said about the league. Other teams have been playing for ages. We've been going seven weeks. We're going to get absolutely battered."

"So?" Rich said. "We expected that."

"Yeah, but hearing it from an actual coach makes it real, doesn't it? Makes it feel a bit..."

"Stupid?" Mike offered.

"I was going to say pointless. But stupid works too."

They sat in silence for a moment, all contemplating the reality of their situation. Four middle-aged men who'd been playing for seven weeks entering a league against people who actually knew what they were doing.

"We're definitely going to come last," Dave said.

"Absolutely last," Mike agreed.

"Embarrassingly last," Rich added.

They looked at each other.

"Still want to do it?" Dave asked.

"Obviously," they all said simultaneously.

In the car park, Rich pulled Steve aside. Again. Dave and Mike pretended not to notice. Again.

"Got that paddle for you," Rich said, pulling a bag from his Porsche. "The Head Evo. Give it a try Saturday."

"Rich, I still don't feel right about this."

"Steve. Mate. It's just sitting in my cupboard. You're actually doing me a favour. Plus—" Rich lowered his voice, but not quite enough "—you were the best of us in there. You've got natural ability. You just need proper equipment to match it."

"I wasn't the best."

"Steve, you did the bandeja. Actually did it. The rest of us nearly killed ourselves trying."

Dave couldn't help but notice Steve's shoulders straighten slightly at this.

"Try it," Rich said. "One session. If you hate it, I'll take it back. No questions asked."

Steve took the bag. "One session."

"That's all I'm asking."

At home, Sarah was reading on the sofa.

"How was the lesson?"

Dave collapsed into the armchair with the dramatic flair of someone who'd been through significant trauma. "Humbling."

"Bad?"

"He basically told us we're all terrible and thinking too much."

"You? Overthinking? Surely not."

"Sarcasm isn't helpful, Sarah."

"What did he say specifically?"

"That I serve like someone who's watched videos but never actually served. That I need to stop thinking and start feeling. That my brain is my enemy."

"Your brain is definitely your enemy."

"Thank you for your support."

"What I mean is—" Sarah put down her book "—you do overthink things. Always have. It's why you're good at your job but terrible at things that require you to just... do."

"I can just do things."

"Dave. You researched microwaves for three weeks."

"That was one time."

"You made a spreadsheet comparing seventeen models."

"Microwaves are an important purchase!"

"They're really not."

Dave pulled out his phone, opened his notes. "He said I need to practice muscle memory. Slow repetition. So I'm going to—"

"Make a schedule?"

"Maybe."

"With specific drills?"

"Possibly."

"Dave."

"What?"

"The coach literally just told you to stop overthinking."

"Planning isn't overthinking. It's being prepared."

Sarah gave him that look. The one that said she loved him but also wanted to shake him.

"Just... try to have fun with it, yeah? That's what it's supposed to be. Fun."

"I am having fun."

"Are you though? Really?"

Dave thought about this. About the stress of serving. The anxiety about league matches. The midnight alarm for court bookings. The hours of YouTube research. The equipment purchases. The constant feeling that he should be better than he was.

"Yes," he said. "Weird fun. Stressful fun. But fun."

"Okay then."

"Is that bad? That it's stressful?"

"Not bad. Just very you."

Later, in bed, Dave tried not to think about Padel. Carlos had said he thought too much. That his brain was his enemy. That he needed to just feel it.

Dave didn't know how to just feel things. He'd spent forty-seven years thinking about things. Analyzing. Planning. Preparing. You couldn't just switch that off.

His phone buzzed. WhatsApp.

Rich, 11:34pm: "Anyone else thinking about what Carlos said?"

Mike, 11:36pm: "About managing expectations?"

Rich, 11:37pm: "About muscle memory. I think we need more practice time."

Dave, 11:39pm: "We're already doing Wednesdays and Saturdays."

Rich, 11:40pm: "What about Sundays?"

Steve, 11:42pm: "Some of us have lives."

Rich, 11:43pm: "Some of us have a league starting in five weeks."

Mike, 11:45pm: "He's got a point."

Dave looked at Sarah, peacefully asleep beside him. Looked at the ceiling. Thought about muscle memory and bad habits and not thinking too much.

Dave, 11:47pm: "Sundays could work. Maybe every other Sunday?"

Mike, 11:48pm: "Yeah okay."

Steve, 11:51pm: "Fine. But only if we go for a pint after."

Rich, 11:52pm: "Deal. Right, I'll book courts."

Dave, 11:53pm: "At midnight?"

Rich, 11:54pm: "When else?"

Dave put his phone down. Picked it up again. Opened YouTube.

Just one more video about serving technique.

Just to check he'd understood what Carlos meant about grip position.

Just to make sure he could practice correctly.

Sarah stirred. "Dave."

"Sorry. Going to sleep now."

"You're on YouTube."

"Just finishing something."

"Padel thing?"

"Maybe."

"Your brain is your enemy."

"The coach said that."

"The coach was right."

Dave closed YouTube. Put his phone on the bedside table. Face down. Screen off.

Lay in the dark trying not to think about serving technique.

His brain, as always, had other ideas.

He thought about serving technique for forty-five minutes before finally falling asleep.

In his dream, Carlos was shaking his head disappointedly while Dave served into the net over and over and over.

"Stop thinking!" Dream Carlos shouted. "Just serve!"

"I'm trying!" Dream Dave shouted back.

"Your trying is thinking! Stop trying! Just do!"

This was, Dave thought even in the dream, absolutely no help at all.

He woke up at 3am with a complete understanding of what he'd been doing wrong with his serve.

He made detailed notes on his phone.

Sarah didn't even bother commenting.

She'd given up.

They'd all given up.

The Padel obsession had won.

Chapter Six

Court Booking Wars

The first casualty of the Padel obsession was Dave's sleep schedule.

ActiveLife Leisure Centre operated on a simple booking system: courts could be reserved exactly seven days in advance. The booking window opened at midnight. This meant that to secure the premium Saturday morning slot at 9am, you needed to be online at midnight the previous Saturday.

Dave's first midnight booking experience was almost spiritual.

He set an alarm for 11:58pm. Sat up in bed. Opened the ActiveLife app. Refreshed. Waited.

11:59pm. Refreshed again.

"What are you doing?" Sarah mumbled.

"Booking courts."

"It's midnight."

"Exactly."

"Dave. Sleep is important."

"So is Saturday morning Padel."

11:59:47pm. Dave's thumb hovered over the refresh button. This was it. This was the moment.

11:59:58pm.

11:59:59pm.

Midnight.

Refresh.

The booking page loaded. Saturday 9am. Available. Dave clicked. Entered details. Payment processing. Loading. Loading.

Success.

"Got it," Dave whispered triumphantly.

"Wonderful. Can we sleep now?"

"In a minute. Just need to book Wednesday."

"Dave."

"And Sunday. Can't forget Sunday."

By 12:07am, Dave had secured all three sessions for the following week. He felt the rush of achievement. The satisfaction of a job well done.

He also felt completely awake.

The WhatsApp group was buzzing.

Rich, 12:03am: "Got all three slots."

Mike, 12:04am: "Same. That was stressful."

Steve, 12:05am: "You're all insane."

Dave, 12:08am: "Successfully booked. That was close though. The Saturday slot almost went."

Rich, 12:09am: "It's getting competitive. More people playing now."

Mike, 12:11am: "Should we book further ahead? Like, multiple weeks?"

Rich, 12:12am: "Can only book seven days out."

Dave, 12:13am: "Unless we get membership. Members can book three weeks ahead."

There was a pause in the chat.

Steve, 12:15am: "How much is membership?"

Rich, 12:16am: "£45/month."

Mike, 12:17am: "That's £540 a year."

Dave, 12:18am: "Plus we're already paying £12 per session per person."

Rich, 12:19am: "If we're playing three times a week, that's £36 per week. Times 52 weeks... £1,872 per year."

Steve, 12:21am: "Jesus Christ."

Mike, 12:22am: "That can't be right."

Dave, 12:23am: "Actually it's only about £1,500 because we won't play every single week. Holidays, Christmas, etc."

Steve, 12:24am: "ONLY £1,500."

Rich, 12:25am: "With membership it'd be £540 plus reduced court fees. Probably save about £400 a year."

Mike, 12:27am: "That's actually not terrible."

Steve, 12:28am: "That's definitely terrible."

Dave, 12:30am: "But if we're committed to this..."

Rich, 12:31am: "Which we are."

Mike, 12:32am: "League and everything."

Dave, 12:33am: "Then maybe membership makes sense?"

Steve, 12:35am: "I hate that you're making sense."

Sarah reached over and took Dave's phone.

"It's past midnight."

"But we're having an important discussion about—"

"Dave. Sleep. Now."

She put the phone on her bedside table. Turned it face down. Gave him a look that suggested this was not negotiable.

Dave lay in the dark, thinking about membership costs and booking systems and whether £540 a year was reasonable for a hobby.

It was quite a lot of money.

But Rich was right. If they were playing three times a week...

"Your brain is very loud," Sarah said. "I can hear you thinking."

"Sorry."

"Go to sleep."

"I'm trying."

"Try harder."

Dave closed his eyes. Tried to quiet his brain. Thought about membership benefits and booking priorities and court availability statistics.

He fell asleep at 1:47am having mentally created a cost-benefit analysis spreadsheet.

The membership discussion continued over the following days.

Rich, unsurprisingly, signed up immediately. "Just makes sense," he declared. "I play four times a week anyway."

Mike was on the fence. "I need to check with Clare. £540 is a lot to commit without discussing it."

Steve was firmly against. "I can barely afford the sessions as they are. Membership is out of the question."

Which left Dave in an awkward middle position. He could afford it. Just. But it seemed excessive for someone who'd only been playing for two months.

"You're actually considering this?" Sarah asked over breakfast.

"Maybe."

"Dave. It's £540."

"Which saves us £400 over the year."

"You've done the maths."

"Of course I've done the maths."

"You've made a spreadsheet."

"Obviously."

Sarah put down her coffee. "Okay. Let me ask you something. In six months, will you still be playing Padel three times a week?"

"Absolutely."

"You're certain?"

"Yes."

"Like you were certain about bread making? And running? And that photography course you did two sessions of?"

"This is different."

"How?"

"I'm actually getting better at it. And we're in a league. And I've made friends."

Sarah softened slightly at this. "You have made friends, haven't you?"

"Yeah. Good ones."

"When was the last time you had a regular thing with mates?"

Dave thought about this. "University?"

"Twenty-five years ago."

"Has it been that long?"

"Dave. If this is genuinely making you happy, and you can afford it, then do it. But don't do it because Rich did it or because you're worried about booking courts at midnight."

"It's not just that."

"What is it then?"

Dave struggled to articulate it. "It's... I don't know. I like having something that's mine. Something I'm working towards. Does that make sense?"

"It makes perfect sense." Sarah reached across the table and took his hand. "Just make sure you're doing it for the right reasons."

"What are the right reasons?"

"Because it makes you happy. Not because it makes you less anxious about booking courts."

This was, Dave realised, a very good point.

He signed up for membership anyway.

The membership card arrived three days later. Plastic. Professional. With his name on it and a barcode that would grant him priority court booking.

Dave felt ridiculously pleased about this.

The WhatsApp group celebrated.

Rich, 10:23am: "Welcome to membership club."

Dave, 10:25am: "Thanks. Feels very official."

Mike, 10:27am: "I'm still thinking about it."

Rich, 10:28am: "What's to think about?"

Mike, 10:29am: "£540."

Steve, 10:31am: "Don't look at me. I'm staying public access."

Rich, 10:33am: "Steve mate, you should at least consider it."

Steve, 10:35am: "With what money?"

There was an awkward pause.

Rich, 10:38am: "Right. Sorry. Wasn't thinking."

Steve, 10:40am: "It's fine. I'm fine with midnight booking wars. Keeps life interesting."

But Dave could tell Steve wasn't fine. Could hear the slight edge in his messages. The reminder that while Rich casually spent money on paddles and memberships, Steve was calculating whether he could afford the £12 session fee.

The first members' booking experience was everything Dave had hoped for.

Sunday night. 9pm. Not midnight. Dave logged into the app with his new membership credentials and booked Saturday morning three weeks in advance.

No stress. No rushing. No refreshing at midnight.

Just smooth, privileged, priority booking.

"This is amazing," he told Sarah.

"It's a booking system."

"It's a PRIORITY booking system."

"Dave. You're getting too excited about this."

"I can book weeks in advance! Look!" He showed her the app. "Saturday the 15th. Saturday the 22nd. Saturday the 29th. All booked. All mine."

"Our money, you mean."

"Our money securing court time for my personal development and social wellbeing."

"That's one way to describe it."

The following Saturday, Dave arrived at ActiveLife with his membership card. Tapped it on the reader at reception. The light went green. The system acknowledged his status.

He was a member now.

Someone who belonged here.

Someone who played Padel three times a week and had priority booking privileges.

"You look pleased with yourself," Steve observed in the changing room.

"Membership card works well."

"Happy for you."

But he didn't sound happy. Sounded tired. A bit worn out.

"You okay?" Dave asked.

"Fine. Just knackered. Been doing extra shifts."

"Extra shifts?"

"Electrician work. Trying to build up a bit of cash. Things are tight."

Dave wanted to ask more but sensed Steve didn't want to talk about it. The changing room went quiet. The kind of quiet that happens when money enters the conversation and nobody knows quite what to say.

Rich burst in, breaking the tension. "Right! Who's ready to absolutely dominate this session?"

"Dominate is strong," Mike said.

"Fine. Who's ready to be slightly less terrible than last week?"

"That I can do."

They played. Dave and Rich with their members' cards and three-week advance bookings. Mike still deciding, still on the fence. Steve with his borrowed paddle and midnight booking slots and extra electrician shifts he didn't talk about.

During the water break, Rich pulled out his phone.

"So," he said casually, "I've been thinking."

"Dangerous," Mike said.

"About Steve's membership situation."

Steve looked up sharply. "I don't have a membership situation."

"Right, but hear me out. What if we—" Rich gestured to Dave, Mike, and himself "—split an additional membership? As a team thing?"

"Rich—" Steve started.

"Wait. Just listen. Four members means four priority bookings. We could use that fourth membership to book courts when we need them. Share it. Like a team resource."

"That's not how it works," Steve said.

"Actually," Dave pulled out his phone, "according to the membership terms, you can have multiple bookings per account. So technically we could all use Rich's membership to book—"

"That's not what I'm suggesting," Rich interrupted. "I'm suggesting we get a fourth membership that Steve uses. Team pays for it. £45 a month split four ways is £11.25 each. Less than a single court session."

Steve's face had gone carefully neutral. "I'm not taking charity."

"It's not charity. It's team investment. You're our best player—"

"I'm not—"

"Steve, you are. You know you are. If you had better booking access, you could practice more. We all benefit from you being better. Therefore, team investment."

The logic was sound but everyone knew what this really was.

Steve knew too.

"No," he said quietly. "Thanks. But no."

"Steve—"

"I said no."

The atmosphere had gone tense. Rich opened his mouth to argue further. Dave caught his eye, shook his head slightly.

Don't push.

They finished the session in slightly awkward silence.

Afterwards, in the car park, Mike pulled Dave aside.

"That was painful."

"Rich means well."

"I know. But Steve's pride..."

"Yeah."

They stood there, two middle-aged men in the February cold, not quite sure how to navigate their friend's financial situation.

"Should we do something?" Mike asked.

"Like what?"

"I don't know. Something that doesn't feel like charity?"

"Good luck with that."

Dave drove home thinking about privilege and pride and how money complicated even the simplest friendships.

At home, he told Sarah about the membership offer.

"That was kind of Rich," she said.

"Steve turned him down."

"Good for Steve."

"Is it though? He could really use the membership. Make his life easier."

"And damage his pride completely? Dave, some people would rather struggle than feel like they're taking hand-outs."

"It's not a handout. It's a team thing."

"From Steve's perspective, it is. Rich has more money than sense, but he needs to be more sensitive about it."

Dave knew she was right. Rich's generosity came from a good place but lacked awareness of how it might land.

That night, he couldn't sleep. Kept thinking about Steve doing extra shifts. About midnight bookings. About the difference between £12 per session being nothing and being something you had to calculate carefully.

At 11:47pm, his phone buzzed.

Steve, private message: "Sorry about earlier. Rich caught me off guard."

Dave, 11:49pm: "No worries. He means well."

Steve, 11:51pm: "I know. I know he does. It's just... complicated."

Dave, 11:53pm: "I get it."

Steve, 11:55pm: "Do you? Not being a dick. Genuinely asking."

Dave thought about this. Did he get it? He'd never had to do extra shifts to afford a hobby. Never had to turn down membership because £540 was impossible rather than uncomfortable.

Dave, 11:58pm: "Probably not. Not really. But I'm trying to."

Steve, 12:01am: "That's more than most people. Thanks."

Dave, 12:03am: "We good?"

Steve, 12:04am: "We're good. See you Wednesday?"

Dave, 12:05am: "Midnight booking?"

Steve, 12:06am: "Midnight booking. Old school."

Dave, 12:07am: "I'll race you."

Steve, 12:08am: "You're on."

Wednesday night, Dave set his alarm for midnight despite having members' priority. Logged in at 11:59pm. Waited.

At midnight exactly, he refreshed. Saw the Wednesday slot appear. Clicked to book.

Message: "This court is already booked."

Dave frowned. Checked. Steve had beaten him by three seconds.

Dave sent a message.

Dave, 12:01am: "You bastard."

Steve, 12:01am: "I'm very fast."

Dave, 12:02am: "You're very competitive."

Steve, 12:03am: "Says the man who made a spreadsheet of our win statistics."

Dave, 12:04am: "That's different. That's data collection."

Steve, 12:05am: "Whatever helps you sleep."

Dave, 12:06am: "Bold of you to assume I sleep."

Dave used his membership to book the following Wednesday instead. But the midnight battle had been fun. Had felt like solidarity somehow.

The group chat buzzed.

Rich, 12:08am: "Did you two just race to book Wednesday?"

Mike, 12:09am: "They absolutely did."

Dave, 12:10am: "Steve won."

Steve, 12:11am: "I'm quite pleased about it."

Rich, 12:13am: "We're all mental."

Mike, 12:14am: "Absolutely certifiable."

Steve, 12:16am: "And yet here we are. Setting midnight alarms to book glass cages."

Dave, 12:17am: "There are worse hobbies."

Rich, 12:18am: "Are there?"

Mike, 12:19am: "Probably not."

Dave lay in bed, Sarah asleep beside him, phone glowing in the dark.

This was absurd. All of it. The midnight bookings. The membership debates. The spreadsheets and YouTube videos and equipment purchases.

But it was also... something.

Friendship, maybe.

Purpose.

A reason to set alarms and make plans and give a shit about something that didn't matter and yet somehow mattered completely.

"Dave," Sarah murmured. "Sleep."

"I am."

"Your phone is on."

"Just finishing something."

"Padel thing?"

"Maybe."

She made a noise that was half amusement, half resignation.

"Love you," he said.

"Love you too. Even though you're ridiculous."

"Because I'm ridiculous."

"That too."

Dave put his phone down. Closed his eyes. Thought about Wednesday's session and Steve's pride and Rich's generosity and Mike's fence-sitting and how four strangers had become something resembling actual friends over a sport they were all still terrible at.

He fell asleep smiling.

His last thought was about Saturday's booking.

Three weeks in advance.

Priority access.

The privilege of membership.

Worth every penny.

Probably.

Chapter Seven
The League Begins

The ActiveLife Beginners' League started on a Saturday in mid-April with all the ceremony of... well, none. No opening speech. No national anthem. Just twelve teams standing around Court 1 looking nervous while a bored receptionist explained the rules.

"Two matches per day," she said, reading from a laminated sheet. "Each match is best of three games to eleven points. You must win by two clear points. Standard Padel rules apply. Any questions?"

Nobody had questions. Everyone looked mildly terrified.

"Great. Match schedule is on the board. Good luck."

She walked off, leaving twelve teams to contemplate their fates.

Dave looked at the bracket. The Rookies were playing first. Against a team called "Smash Bros."

"Smash Bros?" Mike said. "That's... ominous."

"It's probably ironic," Dave suggested. "Like us calling ourselves The Rookies."

"We are rookies though."

"Fair point."

Rich was doing stretches that looked professional. Steve was tapping his borrowed paddle against his shoe with increasing frequency. Dave was trying not to vomit.

"It's just a game," Mike said, clearly trying to convince himself as much as anyone else.

"It's a league match," Dave corrected. "In front of other people. Against a team who probably know what they're doing."

"We know what we're doing."

"Do we though?"

"We know... some things."

"Very specific things."

"Things we learned from YouTube."

"Which may or may not be accurate."

They stood in silence, watching Smash Bros warm up on Court 1. They looked competent. Annoyingly competent. Their serves had purpose. Their returns had spin. They weren't hitting themselves in the face with their paddles.

"We're going to lose," Steve said matter-of-factly.

"Probably," Rich agreed.

"Definitely," Dave added.

"So we're agreed then," Mike said. "Low expectations. Anything above zero points is a victory."

"I'd like to at least return serve once," Dave said.

"Setting the bar nice and low. I respect that."

Their names were called. The Rookies vs Smash Bros. Court 1. Everyone watching.

Dave's legs felt like they'd forgotten how to walk. He made it to the court through sheer willpower and muscle memory.

The Smash Bros were two men who looked to be in their early thirties. Both wearing proper Padel gear. Both looking like they'd done this before.

"First match?" one of them asked, not unkindly.

"That obvious?" Dave said.

"You've got that look. Like you're about to be sick."

"Accurate."

They shook hands. Took positions. Rich and Dave on one side, the two Smash Bros on the other. Mike and Steve watching from the bench, looking equally queasy.

Rich served first.

Actually served. Not just got the ball over the net - actually served with technique and purpose. It bounced in the service box. Hit the back glass. Came back at a difficult angle.

The return was quick. Dave positioned himself. Saw the ball coming. Swung.

Made contact.

The ball went over the net.

The other team returned it. Rich hit it back. They returned again. Dave hit it—

Into the net.

"1-0," someone called.

But they'd had a rally. An actual rally. In a league match. Dave felt absurdly proud.

The game continued. The Smash Bros were better. Significantly better. But not overwhelmingly so. The Rookies were losing points, but they were competing. Occasionally, they even won one.

First game ended 11-4. Respectable. Not good, but respectable.

"We got four points!" Mike said during the break. "That's one more than I expected!"

"The bar was on the floor," Steve pointed out.

"And yet we exceeded it!"

Second game was Mike and Steve's turn. They lost 11-6, which was actually better than Dave and Rich had done.

Steve, it turned out, was genuinely quite good. His serves were accurate. His returns were controlled. He moved around the court with a confidence the rest of them lacked.

"Where did that come from?" Dave asked during the break.

"No idea. It just... works for me."

"You're making the rest of us look bad."

"You're making yourselves look bad. I'm just playing."

Third game was back to Dave and Rich. They lost 11-7.

Match result: 3-0 to Smash Bros. But honestly? Not as humiliating as Dave had feared.

"That was alright actually," Rich said as they came off court.

"We lost three-nil," Mike pointed out.

"But we got seventeen points total. That's... not nothing."

"It's definitely something closer to nothing than something," Steve said.

"Glass half full, Steve."

"Glass is objectively mostly empty."

They watched the next match. Then the one after. By lunchtime, they'd seen six matches and started to understand the hierarchy.

Some teams were genuinely good. Clearly been playing for years, just entering the "beginners" league because they fancied some easy wins.

Some teams were like them. Enthusiastic but limited. Trying their best. Occasionally succeeding by accident.

Some teams were... well, there was one team called "Court Jesters" who didn't seem to understand the rules and argued about every point. They were everyone's favourite to finish last.

"We're not going to be last," Dave observed.

"Aim high," Mike said.

"I'm serious. Court Jesters are terrible. And I reckon 'The Retired' are worse than us too."

"The Retired are all about seventy. That's basically cheating to compare."

"Still counts."

Their second match was at 2pm. Against a team called "Net Results."

Net Results were better than Smash Bros. Significantly better. They had matching shirts. They had a team strategy. They had serves that Dave couldn't even see properly, they came over so fast.

The Rookies lost 3-0 again. This time with only nine total points across the three games.

"That was humbling," Rich said afterwards.

"That was a massacre," Steve corrected.

"Educational massacre?"

"Just a massacre."

They sat on the bench outside Court 1, watching other teams, drinking water that tasted like failure.

"League standings after today," Dave said, checking his phone, "we're joint tenth out of twelve."

"Could be worse," Mike offered.

"How?"

"We could be joint twelfth."

"Next week we play 'The Spin Doctors' and 'Advantage Us.' Both look decent."

"So we'll probably lose both matches."

"Probably."

They sat in contemplative silence.

"Why are we doing this?" Steve asked.

Nobody had an immediate answer.

"Because we're idiots?" Rich suggested.

"Because we paid £45 entry fee?" Mike tried.

"Because we're committed now and can't back out?" Dave offered.

"Because secretly we enjoy it?" Steve said. "Even though we're terrible?"

That felt closest to the truth.

"Yeah," Dave agreed. "That."

In the car park, Rich suggested they go for a pint to debrief.

"Debrief what?" Steve said. "We lost. Twice. Badly."

"Exactly. Need to process the trauma."

They ended up at a pub called The Crown, sitting in the garden despite it being slightly too cold, discussing their performance with the seriousness of professional athletes.

"My serve was off," Rich said.

"Your serve was fine," Dave countered. "My returns were the problem."

"Both our returns were problems," Mike said. "Did you see Steve's serve in the second match though?"

"I saw it," Steve said. "Saw it go into the net."

"Okay but the ones that went over were excellent."

"The ones that went over were adequate."

"Take the compliment, Steve."

"I'll take the compliment when we win a game."

They ordered another round. Then another. By the time they left at 7pm, they'd done a complete tactical analysis of both matches, identified seventeen areas for improvement, and agreed to add a fourth training session per week.

"Monday evenings?" Rich suggested.

"I can do Mondays," Dave said, the beer making him agreeable.

"Mondays work," Mike confirmed.

Steve hesitated. "I've usually got work on Monday evenings."

"How about Tuesday?" Rich tried.

"Tuesdays are worse."

"Wednesday we already have. Thursday?"

"Thursday I could maybe do."

"Right. Thursdays it is then."

So they were now playing four times a week. Wednesday, Thursday, Saturday, Sunday.

Dave got home at 8:30pm, slightly drunk, completely exhausted, and filled with enthusiasm about their league prospects despite having lost both matches.

Sarah was in the kitchen, making dinner.

"How did it go?"

"We lost. Twice."

"Sorry."

"Don't be. We got twenty-six total points across both matches. That's actually quite good considering."

"Considering what?"

"Considering we've been playing for three months."

Sarah turned from the stove. "Dave. You lost. Twice. And you're happy about it?"

"We didn't get destroyed. That's a victory in itself."

"That's... certainly one way to look at it."

"We're adding another training session. Thursdays."

Sarah put down the wooden spoon. "Four times a week?"

"Need to improve before next week's matches."

"Dave. You're playing four times a week?"

"Is that too much?"

"I don't know. Is it?"

Dave thought about this. Four sessions was a lot. That was... what, six hours of Padel per week? Plus travel time. Plus the time spent watching YouTube videos and updating spreadsheets and thinking about technique.

It was basically a part-time job.

"No," Dave said. "It's fine. Completely reasonable."

Sarah gave him that look again. The one that said she knew he was lying but loved him anyway.

"Just promise me you'll still remember you have a family."

"Of course I will!"

"And a job."

"Obviously."

"And other friends."

"I have other friends."

"Do you?"

Dave thought about this. When was the last time he'd seen anyone outside of Padel?

"I have work friends," he tried.

"Work colleagues aren't friends."

"They could be friends."

"But they're not."

"Fine. But I have Mike and Rich and Steve now."

"Who you only see at Padel."

"That's not true. We went to the pub today."

"To talk about Padel."

"To talk about... okay yes, mostly about Padel. But also other things!"

"Like what?"

Dave tried to remember any non-Padel conversation from the pub. They'd definitely talked about... well, there was the discussion about... and that moment when Steve mentioned...

"We talked about beer," Dave said triumphantly.

"Beer."

"Yes. The comparative qualities of different IPAs."

"For how long?"

"Maybe... two minutes?"

"Dave."

"Fine! We talked about Padel the whole time! But that's okay! That's what happens when you have a shared interest! It's bonding!"

Sarah turned back to the stove. "I'm not saying it's bad. I'm just saying... be aware, yeah? Don't let this become your entire life."

"It's not my entire life."

"What did you think about today?"

"Besides Padel?"

"Yes. Besides Padel."

Dave thought about his day. Woke up thinking about the league. Drove to ActiveLife thinking about strategy. Played matches thinking about technique. Went to the pub thinking about improvement. Drove home thinking about next week's matches.

"Work stuff," Dave lied. "Lots of work stuff."

Sarah said nothing. Just kept stirring whatever was in the pot.

Dave knew she was right. Knew the Padel obsession was getting excessive. But he also couldn't quite bring himself to care.

Later, in bed, he checked the league standings on his phone.

Joint tenth out of twelve. Two losses. Twenty-six total points. Goal difference of -28.

Next week: two more matches. Two more chances to not be last.

His phone buzzed. WhatsApp.

Rich, 11:47pm: "Been thinking about today."

Mike, 11:49pm: "And?"

Rich, 11:50pm: "We're not as bad as I thought we'd be."

Steve, 11:52pm: "We lost both matches."

Rich, 11:53pm: "But competitively. We lost competitively."

Dave, 11:55pm: "That's not really a thing."

Rich, 11:56pm: "It should be. We got points. We had rallies. We didn't embarrass ourselves."

Mike, 11:58pm: "The bar is so low it's underground."

Steve, 11:59pm: "And yet we're barely clearing it."

Dave, 12:01am: "Next week we'll do better."

Rich, 12:02am: "Absolutely. Thursday practice session is key."

Mike, 12:03am: "Thursday practice to prepare for Saturday humiliation."

Dave, 12:04am: "The Padel way."

Rich, 12:06am: "Speaking of which, I've been researching doubles tactics."

Steve, 12:07am: "Of course you have."

Rich, 12:08am: "Sending a video. Watch it before Thursday."

Steve, 12:09am: "It's midnight, Rich."

Rich, 12:10am: "So? Perfect time for education."

The video arrived. Seventeen minutes about court positioning and communication in doubles matches. Narrated by a Spanish coach who spoke very quickly.

Dave watched the whole thing.

Obviously.

Made notes.

Obviously.

Created a new section in his spreadsheet: "Doubles Strategy."

Obviously.

Sarah made a noise beside him in the dark.

"Sorry," Dave whispered. "Going to sleep now."

"You're watching Padel videos."

"Just one."

"Dave."

"It's important."

"It's midnight."

"Rich sent it. Would be rude not to watch."

Sarah rolled over, taking most of the duvet with her. "You're impossible."

"I know."

"This obsession is getting worse."

"I know."

"Are you going to do anything about it?"

Dave thought about this. About the league and the training sessions and the midnight bookings and the equipment purchases and the spreadsheets and the YouTube videos and the constant, overwhelming, all-consuming nature of the Padel obsession.

"Probably not," he admitted.

"At least you're honest."

"It's one of my better qualities."

"It's currently your only quality. Everything else is Padel."

"That's not true."

"Name one conversation we've had this week that wasn't about Padel."

Dave thought hard. "We talked about... dinner?"

"To arrange when you'd be home from Padel."

"We discussed... the bathroom?"

"Because you wanted to know if you could install a paddle rack."

"That was a practical question."

"Dave. There's no such thing as a paddle rack."

"There absolutely is. I found them on Amazon."

Sarah sat up, turned on the bedside light. Looked at him with an expression of fond exasperation.

"You're really going to do this, aren't you? The full obsession. The complete commitment. The absolute insanity of it all."

"Apparently."

"Okay then." She turned off the light. "Just... try to stay sane, yeah?"

"I'll do my best."

"And don't forget you have a wife who occasionally likes to see you."

"I could never forget you."

"Even though you spend every waking moment thinking about Padel?"

"Even then."

"Because I'm more important than Padel?"

Dave paused just slightly too long.

"Dave."

"You're definitely more important than Padel."

"You hesitated."

"I didn't hesitate."

"You absolutely hesitated."

"I was gathering my thoughts."

"You were trying to decide if I was more important than Padel."

"That's not— okay, yes, maybe slightly. But I concluded correctly! You are more important!"

Sarah laughed despite herself. "The fact that it was a question is concerning."

"I'm concerned too."

"Good. You should be."

They lay in the dark, Dave's phone glowing slightly on the bedside table where three more WhatsApp messages had just arrived.

"You're not checking those," Sarah said.

"I'm not checking those," Dave agreed.

He checked them at 6:47am the next morning.

Rich had sent two more videos and created a shared Google Doc titled "League Strategy and Improvement Plan."

It was twelve pages long.

Dave read all of it.

Made suggestions.

Added three more pages.

By breakfast time, the document was fifteen pages and covered everything from serving technique to dietary suggestions for optimal performance.

"You've been working on that Padel document, haven't you?" Sarah asked over coffee.

"How did you know?"

"Because I know you. And you have that look."

"What look?"

"The obsessive spreadsheet look. The 'I've been optimising something since 6am' look."

"It's a shared strategy document. Very collaborative."

"It's fifteen pages about hitting a ball in a cage."

"It's fifteen pages about hitting a ball in a cage *correctly*."

"Dave."

"Sarah."

They stared at each other.

"I love you," she said. "But you're absolutely ridiculous."

"I know."

"And this is getting out of hand."

"I know."

"Are you happy though?"

Dave thought about this. About the league matches and the training sessions and the late nights watching YouTube videos. About Rich's generosity and Steve's pride and Mike's constant fence-sitting. About having something to look forward to. About having mates. About having a reason to set alarms and make plans and give a shit.

"Yeah," he said. "I really am."

"Then I guess that's what matters."

"Even though it's ridiculous?"

"Especially because it's ridiculous."

Dave kissed her forehead. "Thank you for tolerating my madness."

"Someone has to."

"I'm lucky it's you."

"Yes. You are."

His phone buzzed. WhatsApp. The group had added six more pages to the document.

It was now twenty-one pages long.

Sarah saw Dave glance at his phone.

"Don't," she said.

"I'm not."

"Dave."

"I'm just checking the time."

"You're checking Padel messages."

"Maybe both."

"Dave!"

But she was smiling. Because she knew. She knew this was who he was. Who they all were. Four middle-aged men who'd found something ridiculous and made it their entire personality.

And somehow, against all odds, it was working.

They were terrible at Padel.

But they were terrible together.

And that made all the difference.

Chapter Eight
The Injury

Dave's elbow started hurting on a Tuesday.

Not dramatically. Not with any particular incident or moment of injury. It just... hurt. A dull ache on the outside of his right elbow that he noticed while typing at work.

He ignored it.

By Wednesday evening, during their training session, the ache had progressed to a sharper pain. Every time he hit the ball, something twinged. Every serve sent a jolt up his arm.

"You alright?" Mike asked during a break.

"Fine. Just a bit sore."

"Sore how?"

"Elbow. It's nothing."

It was definitely something.

By Thursday morning, Dave couldn't properly grip his coffee mug. The pain was constant now. Sharp when he moved, aching when he didn't.

He Googled "elbow pain Padel" at his desk.

The results were not encouraging.

Tennis elbow. Padel elbow. Lateral epicondylitis. Repetitive strain injury. Inflammation of the tendons. Rest required. Possibly for weeks. Possibly for months.

"No," Dave whispered to his screen. "Absolutely not."

He had league matches on Saturday. He had training Thursday evening. He had become someone who played Padel four times a week. He couldn't just... stop.

Dave Googled "how to play Padel with tennis elbow."

The first result: "Don't."

The second result: "Seriously, don't."

The third result: A long article about permanent damage and the importance of rest.

Dave closed his laptop.

He went to Boots at lunch and bought a compression sleeve that promised "targeted support for tennis elbow." The packaging showed a woman playing tennis and smiling like her elbow worked perfectly.

Dave strapped it on in the Boots toilet. It was tight. Uncomfortable. Made his arm look slightly robotic.

He moved his elbow experimentally. It still hurt.

But maybe slightly less?

That evening, he arrived at ActiveLife wearing the compression sleeve under his t-shirt.

"What's that?" Rich asked, pointing at Dave's arm.

"What's what?"

"That bulge under your sleeve."

"Nothing."

"Dave."

"Fine. It's a compression sleeve. My elbow's a bit sore."

"How sore?"

"Bit sore."

"Dave."

"Quite sore. Quite significantly sore."

Rich's face went serious. "You need to rest it."

"It's fine."

"It's clearly not fine if you need a compression sleeve."

"The compression sleeve is preventative."

"That's not what compression sleeves are for."

"How do you know?"

"Because I've had tennis elbow. Twice. You need to rest."

"I'll rest after Saturday."

"Dave—"

"I'm fine. Let's play."

They played. Dave served. His elbow screamed in protest. The ball went wide.

He served again. More pain. Into the net.

Every shot was agony. Every swing sent jolts up his arm. By the end of the session, Dave was serving underarm with less power than a toddler and hitting returns with the enthusiasm of someone actively trying to lose.

"Right," Rich said afterwards. "You're done."

"I'm not done. Saturday we have matches."

"You can barely hold the paddle."

"I can hold it fine."

Dave demonstrated by gripping his paddle. His hand shook. His elbow throbbed. He may have made a small noise of pain.

"Very convincing," Mike said.

"I'm fine."

"You're clearly not fine," Steve added. "You hit yourself in the face with a return because you couldn't control the paddle."

"That was unrelated."

"It was directly related."

They stood in the changing room, three friends looking at Dave with concern, Dave looking at his elbow with betrayal.

"What if I just take it easy on Saturday?" Dave tried. "Light hitting. Nothing intense."

"There's no such thing as light hitting in a league match," Rich said. "You'll try to compete, you'll hurt yourself worse, you'll be out for months instead of weeks."

"You don't know that."

"Yes I do. Because that's exactly what I did. Played through tennis elbow because I didn't want to miss matches. Ended up not playing for three months."

Dave's face must have shown his horror because Rich nodded grimly.

"Three months, Dave. Couldn't pick up a paddle. Could barely pick up a cup of tea. All because I was too stubborn to rest for two weeks."

"Two weeks?"

"If you rest properly. Ice it, compression, anti-inflammatories, no Padel. Two weeks, maybe three. But if you play through it? Could be months. Could be permanent damage."

Dave looked at his paddle. At the court through the changing room window. At everything he'd built over the past three months.

"I'll rest after Saturday," he said quietly.

"Dave—"

"I know. I know you're right. But we've got two matches. We're joint tenth. If we don't play, we forfeit. That's not fair on you three."

"We'll find a substitute," Mike said.

"Who? We don't know anyone else who plays."

"We'll... figure it out. Post on the Facebook group or something."

Dave knew they wouldn't find anyone. Knew they'd forfeit. Knew their league chances would be over before they'd properly begun.

"Let me play Saturday," Dave said. "If it's worse, I'll stop. But let me try."

Rich looked like he wanted to argue. Steve and Mike looked uncertain.

"Fine," Rich said eventually. "But at the first sign it's getting worse, you stop. Promise?"

"Promise."

This was a lie. Dave knew it was a lie. They all knew it was a lie.

But sometimes friendship meant accepting lies because the truth was too uncomfortable.

At home, Dave iced his elbow with a bag of frozen peas. Sarah found him on the sofa, peas wrapped in a tea towel, looking miserable.

"What happened?"

"Elbow."

"How bad?"

"Bit bad."

"Dave."

"Quite bad. Quite significantly bad."

Sarah sat down next to him. "Have you made it worse by playing through it?"

"Maybe."

"Definitely."

"Probably definitely."

"Are you going to rest it?"

"After Saturday."

"Why not before Saturday?"

"League matches. Can't let the team down."

Sarah took the bag of peas, examined his elbow. Even through the compression sleeve, it looked slightly swollen.

"Dave. It's a hobby. It's not worth permanent injury."

"I know that."

"Do you though?"

"Yes! I just... we've worked so hard. Three months of training. Four sessions a week. If I don't play Saturday, we forfeit. That's two automatic losses. Our league hopes are basically over."

"Your league hopes are already basically over. You're joint tenth out of twelve."

"Exactly! We can't afford to forfeit!"

Sarah gave him that look. The one she'd been giving him increasingly frequently lately.

"You're obsessed," she said.

"I'm committed."

"You're going to permanently damage your elbow for a sport you've been doing for three months."

"It won't be permanent."

"You don't know that."

"I'll be careful."

"You're never careful. You're the opposite of careful. You're someone who makes spreadsheets and sets midnight alarms and creates twenty-one page strategy documents. You don't do careful. You do obsessive."

Dave said nothing because she was completely right.

"Just..." Sarah softened slightly. "Please don't hurt yourself. Not for this. It's not worth it."

"It feels worth it."

"I know. That's what worries me."

That night, Dave lay awake, elbow throbbing despite the ibuprofen. He'd read three articles about tennis elbow. Watched two YouTube videos about recovery. Created a spreadsheet tracking his pain levels throughout the day.

His phone buzzed. WhatsApp.

Rich, 11:47pm: "How's the elbow?"

Dave, 11:49pm: "Fine."

Rich, 11:50pm: "Dave. I can tell when you're lying. Even over WhatsApp."

Dave, 11:52pm: "It hurts."

Rich, 11:53pm: "Bad?"

Dave, 11:54pm: "Yeah."

Rich, 11:56pm: "I wasn't joking about the three months. Tennis elbow is serious."

Dave, 11:58pm: "I know."

Rich, 11:59pm: "But you're still playing Saturday."

Dave, 12:01am: "Have to."

Rich, 12:02am: "You really don't."

Dave, 12:04am: "We don't have a substitute. If I don't play, we forfeit. That's not fair on you three."

Rich, 12:06am: "Dave. We'd rather forfeit than have you hurt yourself permanently."

Dave, 12:08am: "You don't mean that."

Rich, 12:09am: "I absolutely mean that. This is supposed to be fun. Not worth injuring yourself over."

Dave stared at his phone. At Rich's message. At the concern from someone who'd started as a stranger and become an actual friend in just three months.

Dave, 12:11am: "I'll see how it feels Saturday morning. If it's bad, I'll pull out."

This was another lie. But it was a lie that let Rich sleep, so maybe it was a kind lie.

Friday, Dave's elbow was worse. Significantly worse. He could barely straighten his arm. Gripping anything caused pain that made his eyes water.

He went to Boots again. Bought stronger ibuprofen. Bought voltarol gel. Bought a different compression sleeve that promised "professional-grade support."

He spent his lunch break in the toilet, applying gel, strapping on the new sleeve, taking pills, and convincing himself this was all perfectly normal behaviour.

Priya from Accounts saw him emerging.

"You alright?"

"Fine. Just... elbow thing."

"You've been walking funny all week."

"Have I?"

"Like you're cradling an injured bird."

This was unfortunately accurate.

"It's nothing. Just need to rest it."

"So you're resting it?"

"After tomorrow."

"Why after tomorrow?"

"League match."

Priya looked at him the way everyone had been looking at him lately. Like he'd lost his mind and they were watching it happen in real-time.

"Is it worth it?" she asked.

"I don't know," Dave admitted. "But I'm doing it anyway."

Saturday morning arrived with all the joy of dental surgery.

Dave's elbow was purple. Actually purple. Bruised and swollen and throbbing with a pain that suggested his body was actively trying to tell him something important.

He ignored his body.

He'd gotten quite good at ignoring his body lately.

Sarah found him in the bathroom, applying more voltarol gel.

"Dave. Your elbow is purple."

"It's fine."

"It's purple."

"Purplish. Barely noticeable."

"Dave. You can't play like this."

"I'll be careful."

"There's no such thing as careful when you're obsessed."

"I'm not—" He stopped. Looked at his purple elbow. At the compression sleeves and pain gel and pills. At himself in the mirror, a forty-seven-year-old man about to play sport with an injury that clearly required rest. "Okay. Maybe I'm slightly obsessed."

"Slightly?"

"Moderately."

"Dave."

"Fine. Completely. Utterly. Absolutely obsessed. Happy?"

"Not really. Because you're still going to play."

"I have to."

"You really don't."

"If I don't, we forfeit."

"So forfeit!"

"I can't do that to them."

Sarah looked at him for a long moment. "You know what the crazy thing is? They wouldn't want you to do this. They'd tell you to rest."

"I know."

"But you're doing it anyway."

"I am."

"Because you're obsessed."

"Because I'm committed."

"That's the same thing."

"It's really not."

"Dave. Just..." She kissed his forehead. "Try not to make it worse, okay? And if it gets bad, stop. Actually stop. Not 'I'll stop in five minutes' stop. Actually stop."

"I promise."

This was probably a lie too.

At ActiveLife, the other three took one look at Dave's face and knew.

"It's bad," Mike said.

"It's fine."

"Dave—"

"I'm playing. Let's not discuss it."

"Dave, mate—" Rich started.

"I said let's not discuss it."

Steve was quiet. Just watching. Then: "If you make it worse, you're an idiot."

"Noted."

"I'm serious. This is the dumbest thing you could do."

"Also noted."

"But you're doing it anyway."

"Correct."

"You're an idiot."

"We've established that."

They took the court for their first match. Against a team called "The Baseline Bandits" who looked professional and moved like they'd been playing for years.

Dave served. His elbow screamed. The ball went over. Barely. With no power. No spin. Nothing.

The return came fast. Dave positioned himself. Swung. His elbow gave out mid-swing. The paddle flew from his hand, clattered against the glass wall, fell to the ground.

There was a moment of silence.

"You alright?" one of the Baseline Bandits asked.

"Fine. Just... grip slipped."

Dave picked up his paddle. Served again. Made it over. Three shots later, his elbow failed again. This time he managed to keep hold of the paddle but the ball went straight into the net.

They lost the first game 11-1. Dave had caused ten of those lost points.

During the break, Rich pulled him aside.

"You need to stop."

"I'm fine."

"You're not fine. You can't grip the paddle properly."

"Just warming up."

"Dave. Please. Stop before you do permanent damage."

Dave looked at the court. At Mike and Steve waiting. At the Baseline Bandits looking concerned. At his purple, throbbing, actively-rebelling elbow.

"One more game," he said.

"Dave—"

"One more. If it's not better, I'll stop."

It was not better.

It was significantly worse.

By the third point, Dave couldn't serve at all. Just dropped the ball and hoped it went over. It didn't. By the fifth point, he couldn't return anything. Just stood there, paddle hanging limply, while balls flew past him.

They lost 11-0.

"Right," Rich said firmly. "That's it. You're done."

Dave wanted to argue. Wanted to insist he could continue. Wanted to prove he wasn't letting the team down.

But he couldn't even lift his paddle anymore.

"Sorry," he said quietly.

"Don't apologise," Mike said. "Just go home and rest that thing before it falls off."

"We've got another match at two."

"We'll forfeit. Or find someone. Doesn't matter. You need to go home."

"But—"

"Dave. Go home."

Steve put a hand on his shoulder. "You tried. You're an idiot, but you tried. Now go before you make it worse."

Dave drove home one-handed, right arm cradled against his chest, feeling like the world's biggest failure.

Sarah was in the garden, reading.

"You're home early."

"Couldn't play."

"Good."

"We lost eleven-one and then eleven-nil."

"I don't care about that. I care about your elbow."

Dave sat down heavily in the garden chair. His elbow throbbed. His pride throbbed worse.

"I let them down," he said.

"You tried to play through an injury. That's not letting them down. That's being stupid, but not letting them down."

"Same thing."

"Not even close."

Dave's phone buzzed. WhatsApp. Group chat.

He expected anger. Disappointment. Frustration that he'd played badly and wasted their Saturday.

Mike, 10:47am: "Just forfeit the second match. Not worth getting a random substitute."

Rich, 10:49am: "Agreed. Dave, hope the elbow's okay. Get it looked at properly."

Steve, 10:51am: "Seriously. Doctor. Physiotherapist. Whatever. Just sort it."

Mike, 10:52am: "We don't care about the league. Well, we do. But not as much as we care about you not being permanently injured."

Rich, 10:54am: "We're 10th out of 12 anyway. Couple more losses won't change anything."

Steve, 10:55am: "Plus we'll probably lose even with you. So really you're just saving us from slightly bigger losses."

Dave, 10:57am: "Sorry."

Mike, 10:58am: "Stop apologising."

Rich, 10:59am: "Just rest it. Properly. Weeks, not days."

Dave, 11:01am: "What about training sessions?"

Rich, 11:02am: "What about them?"

Dave, 11:03am: "Wednesday? Thursday?"

Steve, 11:04am: "Dave. You're benched. Doctor's orders. Well, our orders. But same thing."

Mike, 11:05am: "We'll train without you. You'll watch from the side and give unhelpful advice."

Dave, 11:06am: "That sounds awful."

Rich, 11:07am: "Agreed. But better than permanent injury."

Dave put his phone down. Looked at his purple elbow. At Sarah watching him with concern and exasperation.

"They're not angry," he said, surprised.

"Why would they be angry?"

"I played badly. Cost us matches. Let them down."

"You tried to play through an injury because you didn't want to let them down. That's not the same as actually letting them down."

"Feels the same."

"Feelings aren't facts."

Dave sat in the garden, cradling his injured elbow, feeling sorry for himself in that very specific way that men do when they've been stupid and are now facing consequences.

"How long until I can play again?" he asked.

"Probably weeks."

"Weeks?"

"If you rest properly."

"How many weeks?"

"Two? Three? Four? Depends on how bad it is."

Dave did the maths. Four weeks meant missing twelve sessions. Twelve sessions meant... actually, he couldn't calculate what that meant. But it felt catastrophic.

"What will I do?" he said.

"Live your life?"

"I mean... what will I do on Wednesday evenings? And Thursday? And Saturday mornings? And Sunday afternoons?"

"Dave. You have a life outside Padel."

"Do I?"

They looked at each other.

"Alright," Sarah admitted. "Maybe you don't anymore. But this is a chance to remember what that life looks like."

"What if I don't like it?"

"Then you're really in trouble."

Dave went to the doctor on Monday. Confirmed tennis elbow. Actually, the doctor said "lateral epicondylitis" which sounded more serious and therefore more impressive when explaining to people why he couldn't play.

"Rest," the doctor said. "Ice. Anti-inflammatories. No repetitive movements with that arm."

"For how long?"

"Four to six weeks."

Dave's face must have shown his devastation because the doctor softened slightly.

"I know it seems like a long time. But trust me, if you try to play through it, you'll make it worse. Could be months. Could be permanent. Rest now, play later. Don't play now, regret forever."

"That's quite poetic."

"I see a lot of sports injuries. Got good at the motivational speeches."

Dave left with a prescription for stronger anti-inflammatories and instructions to do absolutely nothing with his right arm for at least a month.

The first week of not playing was torture.

Wednesday evening, Dave drove to ActiveLife anyway. Sat in the viewing area above Court 2. Watched the other three play without him.

They were... fine. Not great. They lost to a random fourth player they'd found from the Facebook group. But they were functional. They didn't actually need Dave.

This should have been comforting.

It was somehow worse.

Thursday he did the same thing. Sat in the viewing area, watching, feeling useless.

"You know you don't have to come, right?" Mike said afterwards.

"I know."

"But you're coming anyway."

"Apparently."

"That's quite sad."

"I'm aware."

Saturday, Dave watched both league matches from the stands. They lost both. Badly. The substitute they'd found was terrible. Actually worse than Dave, which was almost impressive.

"Missing you out there," Rich said.

"You're just being nice."

"I'm really not. You're better than Random Facebook Dave."

"Random Facebook Dave hit himself in the face. Twice."

"Exactly. You only do that once per session."

Dave smiled despite himself.

Sunday, he watched again. Couldn't quite bring himself to stay home. Sat in the viewing area, cradling his elbow, watching his friends play without him.

"This is pathetic," he told Sarah that evening.

"Bit pathetic," she agreed.

"I'm watching other people play sport instead of living my life."

"Yes."

"That's really quite sad."

"Very sad."

"Should I stop?"

"Probably."

"Will I stop?"

"Definitely not."

Sarah was right. Dave continued to attend every session, sitting in the viewing area like the world's saddest spectator.

But something shifted in those weeks.

Watching from the outside, Dave started to notice things. How Rich was actually quite good but tried too hard. How Mike was improving but didn't realise it. How Steve was clearly the most talented but seemed almost embarrassed by it.

He made notes. Created a new spreadsheet. "Observation Analysis."

By week three, Dave had seventeen pages of notes about technique, positioning, and strategy.

"You know," Mike said after a Thursday session, "you're actually more useful from the stands than on court."

"That's definitely not true."

"No seriously. You spotted that thing with my footwork. I've been doing it wrong for weeks and nobody noticed."

"It was obvious from up there."

"Maybe you should stay injured. Be our coach."

"Absolutely not."

But Dave had to admit, there was something satisfying about the analysis. About seeing patterns. About helping his friends improve.

By week four, his elbow was significantly better. The purple had faded. The pain had reduced to a dull ache. He could grip things again.

The doctor cleared him to "light activity."

Dave interpreted this as "full Padel session."

The doctor clarified: "Light activity means gentle move-ment. Not competitive sport."

"Padel isn't competitive."

"You're in a league."

"A beginners' league."

"Still a league."

"Very gentle league."

The doctor looked at him with the weariness of someone who knew he was fighting a losing battle.

"Fine. One session. Gentle hitting. No serves. No compet-itive play. If it hurts, stop immediately. Understood?"

"Absolutely."

Dave's first session back was a Wednesday evening in late May.

He arrived at Court 2 feeling nervous. The paddle felt for-eign in his hand. The court looked different. Everything felt slightly off.

"Take it easy," Rich reminded him. "Just gentle rallies."

"Just gentle rallies," Dave agreed.

They started hitting. Soft shots. No power. Just getting a feel for it again.

And it felt... amazing. His elbow twinged slightly but nothing serious. The ball connected with the sweet spot. The paddle responded. Everything worked.

"How's it feeling?" Mike asked.

"Good. Really good."

"Don't overdo it."

"I won't."

Dave absolutely overdid it.

Within twenty minutes he was hitting full power. Serving. Competing. Forgetting entirely about his injury in the joy of actually playing again.

His elbow held up. Mostly. There was some pain. But manageable pain. Acceptable pain.

By the end of the session, Dave was grinning like an idiot.

"That was brilliant," he said.

"Your elbow okay?" Steve asked.

"Perfect."

"It's not perfect though, is it?"

"Fine. It hurts a bit. But good hurt. Exercise hurt."

"That's not a thing."

"It is now."

Saturday, Dave played his first league match since the injury. Four weeks of watching. Four weeks of analysis. Four weeks of pent-up enthusiasm.

They played against "The Smash Bros" again. The team they'd played in week one.

And they won.

Not the match. They lost 2-1. But they won a game. An actual game. 11-9.

"WE WON A GAME!" Mike shouted, loud enough that several other courts turned to look.

"It's one game," Dave said, but he was grinning.

"IT'S ONE MORE THAN ZERO GAMES!"

"That maths checks out."

They celebrated like they'd won Wimbledon. High fives. Chest bumps. Rich may have done a small victory dance.

The Smash Bros looked confused but happy for them.

"First league game win?" one of them asked.

"Yes!"

"Congratulations. That's a big moment."

"It really is."

And it was. After four months of playing, twelve weeks of league matches, countless training sessions, one injury, and approximately seventy-three YouTube videos, they'd won a game.

Not a match. A game.

But it was progress.

And progress, Dave had learned, was what mattered.

That night, Dave's elbow throbbed. Properly throbbed. He probably had overdone it. Probably should have rested more. Probably should have listened to everyone's advice.

But they'd won a game.

And that made everything worth it.

Probably.

Chapter Nine

The Wives

The dinner was Sarah's idea.

"I want to meet them," she said one evening in early June.

"Meet who?"

"The wives. Partners. Whatever. The other people whose lives have been taken over by this Padel nonsense."

Dave looked up from his phone where he'd been reviewing match statistics. "That's a bit dramatic."

"Dave. You play four times a week. You watch YouTube videos at midnight. You have a spreadsheet with forty-seven tabs. Your browser history is just 'Padel technique' and 'best paddles under £200' and 'how to improve serve accuracy.' This is taking over your life. I want to commiserate with the other casualties."

"We're not casualties."

"Dave. Last week you dreamed about court positioning and woke me up to discuss it."

"That was important tactical insight."

"It was 3am."

"Insights don't operate on a schedule."

Sarah gave him that look. The one she'd perfected over their years together. The one that said she loved him but also wanted to shake him.

"Dinner," she said firmly. "This Saturday. You four, us four. Somewhere nice. We're going to meet properly and discuss what to do about your collective mental health crisis."

"It's not a mental health crisis."

"You're right. It's worse. It's a hobby."

Dave knew better than to argue. "I'll mention it to the group."

He mentioned it to the group.

Dave, 8:47pm: "Sarah wants to organise a dinner. Us four plus partners. Saturday night."

There was a pause in the chat.

Mike, 8:52pm: "Oh god."

Rich, 8:53pm: "That sounds civilised."

Steve, 8:55pm: "I don't have a partner."

Mike, 8:56pm: "What about Emma?"

Steve, 8:57pm: "We went on three dates. That was two months ago."

Rich, 8:58pm: "What happened?"

Steve, 9:00pm: "I may have talked about Padel too much."

Mike, 9:01pm: "How much is too much?"

Steve, 9:02pm: "Apparently the entire third date."

Dave, 9:04pm: "The ENTIRE date?"

Steve, 9:05pm: "I thought she was interested. She asked questions."

Rich, 9:06pm: "She was being polite, mate."

Steve, 9:07pm: "I realised that. Eventually. Around the time she stopped replying to my messages."

Mike, 9:09pm: "So no Emma then."

Steve, 9:10pm: "No Emma."

Rich, 9:11pm: "Come anyway. Even numbers are overrated."

Steve, 9:13pm: "Sure. Why not. I'll be the sad single one while you're all coupled up talking about how terrible we are."

Dave, 9:15pm: "They won't talk about how terrible we are."

Mike, 9:16pm: "They absolutely will."

Rich, 9:17pm: "That's definitely the entire point of this dinner."

Dave, 9:18pm: "Fine. They'll talk about how terrible we are. But at least there'll be food."

Saturday evening arrived with the kind of nervous energy usually reserved for job interviews or dental appointments.

They'd booked a table at an Italian restaurant called Oliveto. Mid-range. Nice enough to feel like effort, not so fancy that anyone felt uncomfortable.

Dave and Sarah arrived first. Then Mike and Clare. Clare was a geography teacher at the same school as Mike. Short, efficient-looking, with the kind of patient expression that suggested she dealt with teenagers and therefore couldn't be fazed by much.

"So you're Clare," Sarah said, shaking hands. "I've heard a lot about you."

"All lies," Clare said. "Whatever Mike told you, assume the opposite."

"I told her you were understanding about my Padel schedule," Mike protested.

"I said I was accepting. Understanding suggests I comprehend why a grown man needs to play tennis in a cage four times a week."

"It's not tennis."

"So you keep saying."

They sat down. Ordered drinks. Made small talk about work and the weather and literally anything except Padel.

Rich and Camilla arrived next. Camilla was exactly what Dave had pictured - polished, well-dressed, with the slightly bored expression of someone who was used to her husband having various enthusiasms.

"Richard tells me you've all become quite serious about this," she said, sitting down.

"It's Rich," Rich corrected automatically.

"You'll always be Richard to me, darling."

"See what I live with?" Rich said to the table.

"Oh, you poor thing. The woman who tolerates your countless hobbies and expensive purchases. How terrible for you."

"I don't have countless hobbies."

"You have seven paddles."

"I have four paddles. Three were investments."

"In what? The Padel futures market?"

The table laughed. Rich looked vaguely embarrassed.

"See?" Camilla said to Sarah. "He's incorrigible."

"Dave has a spreadsheet with forty-seven tabs," Sarah offered.

"Mike watches training videos during breakfast," Clare added.

"Richard bought a book about Padel tactics," Camilla said. "A book. Like it's something academic."

"It IS academic," Rich protested. "It's about game theory and strategic positioning—"

"It's about hitting a ball in a glass box, darling."

Steve arrived last, alone, looking slightly uncomfortable.

"Sorry. Couldn't find parking."

"Couldn't find a date either?" Rich said, then immediately looked mortified. "Sorry. That came out wrong."

"It's fine. I'm very single and very okay with it."

"We're glad you're here," Sarah said warmly. "Someone needs to balance out the couple energy."

"Happy to be the token single."

They ordered food. The conversation flowed surprisingly easily. The wives - Sarah, Clare, and Camilla - clearly had a lot to say about their partners' new obsession.

"The midnight bookings," Clare said. "That's what gets me. Mike sets an alarm. For midnight. To book sports courts."

"Dave does the same thing," Sarah said. "I thought he was having an affair. Turned out he was just being weird about Padel."

"Which is worse?" Mike asked.

"Debatable," Clare said.

"At least an affair would be exciting," Sarah mused.

"I'm right here," Dave said.

"We know, darling. That's the problem."

Camilla sipped her wine. "Richard's thing is the equipment. Seven paddles. For one sport. That he's been doing for five months."

"Four paddles," Rich corrected. "And they're all different."

"They absolutely are not all different."

"This one's for power, this one's for control, this one's for—"

"For spending money unnecessarily?"

"For varied playing conditions!"

"It's an indoor court. The conditions are identical every week."

The table laughed again. Rich looked at Dave for support.

"I only have one paddle," Dave said.

"Yes but you have a spreadsheet with forty-seven tabs," Sarah reminded him.

"Forty-eight now. I added a nutrition tracking sheet."

"Why?" Clare asked.

"Optimal performance requires optimal fuel."

"It's hitting a ball."

"It's hitting a ball CORRECTLY."

The food arrived. Pasta for most of them. Pizza for Rich, who apparently had specific carbohydrate requirements pre-training.

"Pre-training?" Camilla said. "It's Saturday night. When are you training?"

"Sunday morning at ten."

"That's fourteen hours away."

"Digestion takes time."

Camilla looked at Sarah and Clare. "Do you see what I deal with?"

"At least yours is wealthy," Clare said. "Mine spends money we don't have on coaching sessions."

"They're investments," Mike protested.

"In what? Your future professional Padel career?"

"Maybe."

"Mike. You're forty-nine years old and you teach geography."

"Lots of professional athletes started late."

"Name one."

Mike thought hard. "There must be some."

"There aren't."

"What about that bowls player who—"

"Bowls doesn't count."

"Why not?"

"Because it's bowls."

Steve had been quiet, eating his pizza, watching the couples bicker with the amusement of someone who wasn't involved.

"What about you, Steve?" Sarah asked. "No one giving you grief about Padel?"

"Benefits of being single. No one to complain to."

"Or to support you," Camilla added gently.

"Or that. But also no one to tell me I'm being ridiculous."

"You are being ridiculous though," Clare said. "You all are. Four times a week. Midnight bookings. Strategy documents. Group chats at 2am discussing serving technique. This is insane behaviour."

"It's enthusiastic behaviour," Dave corrected.

"It's obsessive behaviour," Sarah said. "Let's call it what it is."

The four men looked at each other. Some kind of silent communication passed between them.

"Okay," Rich admitted. "Maybe it's slightly obsessive."

"Slightly?" Camilla said.

"Fine. Quite obsessive. Possibly very obsessive."

"Definitely very obsessive," Mike added.

"Borderline pathological," Dave contributed.

"But—" Steve held up a hand "—it makes us happy."

There was a pause.

"Does it though?" Clare asked, not unkindly. "You all seem quite stressed about it."

"That's just competitive stress," Rich said.

"You're joint ninth out of twelve teams."

"Exactly. We could be tenth. The stress is real."

Sarah leaned forward. "Can I ask a serious question?"

"Uh oh," Dave muttered.

"Why this? Why Padel? Why now? What is it about hitting a ball in a glass cage that's made you all lose your minds?"

The four men looked at each other again.

Mike spoke first. "It's... something that's ours, I suppose. I teach teenagers all day. Go home. Mark homework. Plan lessons. Sleep. Repeat. Padel is the only thing I do that's just for me."

Clare's expression softened slightly.

Rich nodded. "I work all the time. Build developments, manage properties, endless meetings. This is the only thing I do that isn't about money. It's just... playing. When was the last time any of us just played?"

"University," Dave said. "Maybe earlier."

"Exactly. We're all so busy being adults. Being responsible. Being sensible. This is permission to be a bit silly."

Steve was quiet. Then: "It's nice having mates, isn't it?"

The table went quiet.

"I moved here three years ago," Steve continued. "After the divorce. Didn't know anyone. Worked. Went home. Worked some more. I wasn't... lonely exactly. But I wasn't not lonely. And then one Saturday I tried this stupid Spanish cage tennis thing, and now I have people who send me videos at midnight and create spreadsheets about my serving technique and genuinely care whether I'm okay."

He stopped, looked down at his plate.

"Sorry. That got a bit heavy."

"Don't apologise," Sarah said quietly. "That's... that's actually really lovely."

Dave looked at Steve. At this man who'd arrived with a borrowed paddle and gradually become one of his closest friends. Who'd never mentioned being lonely. Who'd hidden behind jokes and banter.

"You never said," Dave said.

"You never asked."

"Would you have told us?"

Steve considered this. "Probably not. But you included me anyway. That's what mattered."

Camilla dabbed at her eyes. "Okay. This has taken an unexpected turn."

"Right," Clare said, voice slightly thick. "So. What you're saying is, this ridiculous obsession has actually been... good for you?"

"Surprisingly good," Mike admitted.

"Weirdly good," Rich agreed.

"Life-changingly good," Dave added.

"Annoyingly good," Steve finished. "Because now I can't just casually stop. You've made me care about something."

"Bastards," Mike said.

"Complete bastards," Rich agreed.

They sat in silence for a moment, four middle-aged men and their long-suffering partners, in an Italian restaurant on a Saturday night, having accidentally had a meaningful conversation.

"Well," Sarah said eventually. "I suppose we can't object to something that makes you happy and gives you friends."

"We can still object to the midnight bookings though," Clare added.

"And the forty-eight tab spreadsheets," Camilla contributed.

"And the constant Padel chat," Sarah finished.

"Fair," Dave said.

The conversation moved on. Lighter topics. Work gossip. Holiday plans. The usual dinner party safe ground.

But something had shifted. The wives - Sarah, Clare, and Camilla - seemed less exasperated and more understanding. Not accepting, exactly. But aware that this stupid hobby had given their partners something important.

Over dessert, Camilla asked about the league standings.

"Joint ninth," Rich said. "One win, ten losses."

"That's not great."

"That's terrible. But we won a game two weeks ago. An actual game. 11-9."

"Congratulations?"

"It was a big moment. We celebrated for approximately three hours."

"Over winning one game?"

"It was our first!"

Sarah looked at Dave. "You didn't tell me that."

"Didn't I?"

"No. You came home, iced your elbow, and went to bed at 9pm."

"Oh. Right. I was quite tired."

"But you won. Your first league game. That's actually significant."

"It's one game."

"But it's progress. And you're always going on about progress."

Dave felt something warm in his chest. Sarah understood. Not the Padel part - she'd never understand the Padel part. But the achievement part. The working towards something and seeing results part.

"Yeah," he said. "It was pretty great."

"Even if you're still joint ninth out of twelve?"

"Even then."

After dinner, they stood outside the restaurant, saying goodbyes, promising to do this again.

"This was nice," Clare said. "I mean, I still think you're all mad. But nice."

"We should do it monthly," Camilla suggested. "Keep everyone grounded."

"Monthly?" Rich said. "That seems excessive."

"Says the man with seven paddles."

"Four paddles!"

They laughed, separated into their respective cars, drove home to their respective lives.

In Dave and Sarah's car, heading back through Saturday night traffic, Sarah said: "They seem nice."

"They are. Really good lads."

"Steve's lonely."

"I didn't realise."

"Men never do."

"Is that a man thing?"

"It's definitely a man thing. You're all terrible at admitting feelings."

"We have a group chat."

"Where you discuss serving technique. That doesn't count."

Dave thought about this. "We should do more stuff. Beyond Padel."

"Like what?"

"I don't know. Pub? Cinema? Normal friend stuff?"

"Dave. You can barely fit four Padel sessions into your week. When exactly would you do normal friend stuff?"

"After Padel?"

"So... more Padel-adjacent socialising?"

"I suppose."

"You're hopeless."

"I know."

But Dave was already thinking about it. About Steve being lonely. About Rich throwing himself into hobbies to avoid thinking about what? About Mike teaching teenagers and marking homework and maybe feeling a bit lost.

About himself, forty-seven years old, making spreadsheets at midnight because it gave him purpose.

At home, getting ready for bed, Dave said: "Thanks for organising tonight."

"It was good, wasn't it?"

"Really good. I think they needed it."

"You all needed it. To remember there's more to life than Padel."

"Is there though?"

Sarah threw a pillow at him.

"Okay, okay. There's more to life than Padel."

"Is there?"

"Definitely. Probably. Maybe."

"Dave."

"Fine. There's you. And the kids. And work. And... other stuff."

"Very convincing."

"I'm working on it."

He got into bed, checked his phone out of habit. The WhatsApp group was buzzing.

Rich, 11:34pm: "That was nice."

Mike, 11:36pm: "Better than expected."

Steve, 11:38pm: "Thanks for including me. Even though I was the sad single."

Rich, 11:40pm: "You're not sad. You're selectively single."

Steve, 11:41pm: "That's a nice way of saying no one will date me because I talk about Padel too much."

Mike, 11:43pm: "Have you tried not talking about Padel?"

Steve, 11:44pm: "What else would I talk about?"

Dave, 11:46pm: "That's actually a good question."

Rich, 11:47pm: "We should probably develop other interests."

Mike, 11:48pm: "Or just lean into the Padel thing completely."

Steve, 11:49pm: "I vote lean in."

Dave, 11:50pm: "Same."

Rich, 11:51pm: "Unanimous then. We're Padel people now."

Mike, 11:52pm: "Is that sad?"

Rich, 11:53pm: "Probably."

Steve, 11:54pm: "Definitely."

Dave, 11:55pm: "But we're okay with it."

Mike, 11:56pm: "Weirdly okay with it."

Rich, 11:57pm: "Right. See you Sunday morning. 10am."

Dave, 11:58pm: "Sunday morning. Can't wait."

Sarah reached over, took his phone, put it on her bedside table.

"Sleep," she said.

"Just finishing—"

"Dave. They'll still be there tomorrow."

"I know. But—"

"Sleep."

Dave closed his eyes. Thought about dinner. About Steve's admission. About Rich's expensive hobbies and Mike's need for something that was his. About four strangers who'd met in a glass cage and somehow become friends.

About Sarah and Clare and Camilla, who tolerated the madness because they understood, somewhere deep down, that sometimes middle-aged men needed silly hobbies and midnight group chats and reasons to set alarms.

His phone buzzed on Sarah's bedside table.

Another message. Probably Rich sending a video. Or Mike creating a new shared document. Or Steve making a joke about being single.

"Leave it," Sarah said.

"I'm leaving it."

"You're thinking about looking at it."

"Only a bit."

"Dave."

"Fine. I'm sleeping."

He was asleep within minutes, dreaming about Padel and friendship and Italian restaurants where everyone understood everyone else, even when they pretended not to.

The WhatsApp message stayed unread until 6:47am the next morning.

It was Rich, sending a thirteen-minute video about advanced serving techniques.

Dave watched the whole thing while making coffee.

Sarah appeared in the kitchen doorway.

"Padel video?"

"Maybe."

"At 6am on a Sunday?"

"Best time for learning. Brain's fresh."

"Your brain is never fresh. Your brain is consumed by Padel."

"Accurate."

She poured herself coffee. Sat at the kitchen table. Looked at him with that expression that was equal parts affection and resignation.

"You're genuinely happy though, aren't you?"

"Yeah," Dave said. "I really am."

"Even though you're terrible at it?"

"Especially because I'm terrible at it. Gives me room to improve."

"Always the optimist."

"Always the spreadsheet maker."

"Same thing really."

They sat in the morning quiet, drinking coffee, Dave's phone showing a paused video of serving technique, Sarah reading the news on her iPad.

Normal. Comfortable. Home.

Just with slightly more Padel than before.

Significantly more Padel, actually.

But that was okay.

That was life now.

And life, surprisingly, was pretty good.

Chapter Ten
The Holiday

Dave had booked the Cornwall holiday back in January. Two weeks in a cottage near St Ives. Family time. Beaches. Pasties. The kind of traditional British summer holiday where you pretended the rain was atmospheric.

That was before Padel.

Now, in late July, as they loaded the car for the journey, Dave was having very specific concerns.

"How far is St Ives from the nearest Padel court?" he asked Sarah, who was trying to fit seventeen beach towels into an already-full boot.

"I don't know."

"Could you check?"

"Dave. We're on holiday."

"I know. Just curious."

"You're not just curious."

"I might want to play once or twice."

"Dave."

"What? It's two weeks. That's eight missed sessions. My serve accuracy will suffer."

Sarah straightened up from the boot, looked at him with an expression that suggested she was reconsidering their entire marriage.

"Dave. We're going on a family holiday. With your children. Who you haven't seen properly in months because you're always playing Padel. You are not playing Padel in Cornwall."

"What if there's a court nearby?"

"There won't be."

"But what if there is?"

"Then you'll walk past it. Like a normal person. And spend time with your family."

"I can do both."

"You really can't."

The kids arrived downstairs. Tom and Emily, home from university for the summer, looking like they'd rather be anywhere else.

"Everyone ready?" Dave asked with forced enthusiasm.

"Thrilled," Emily said in a tone that suggested the opposite.

"Cornwall's great!" Dave tried. "Beaches, surfing, cream teas—"

"Padel courts?" Tom said innocently.

Sarah glared at Dave. "You told them."

"I may have mentioned it."

"Dave. You promised."

"I promised I'd prioritise family time. Which I will. But if there happens to be a court nearby—"

"There won't be."

There were three courts. In Truro. Forty minutes from St Ives.

Dave discovered this during the drive down, while Sarah was driving and couldn't confiscate his phone.

"Found one," he announced.

"Found what?" Sarah asked, eyes on the motorway.

"Nothing. Just... a thing."

"A Padel thing?"

"Maybe."

"Dave."

"Three courts. Indoor facility. Good reviews. Very reasonable hourly rate."

"Dave, I swear to god—"

"I'm just researching! Knowledge is power!"

"Knowledge is annoying," Emily said from the back seat.

"You're not playing," Sarah said firmly. "We're having family time. Proper family time. No Padel. No midnight bookings. No YouTube videos. Just us, the beach, and normal human interaction."

"I'm very good at normal human interaction."

"You spent last Tuesday's dinner explaining court positioning to Tom."

"He was interested!"

"I fell asleep," Tom confirmed. "Literally fell asleep at the dinner table."

"That was rude."

"Dad, you'd been talking for forty-five minutes."

"It was comprehensive."

They arrived at the cottage at 6pm. It was perfect. Exposed beams. Sea views. Kitchen that opened onto a garden with a BBQ. Everything you'd want from a Cornwall holiday cottage.

Dave unpacked methodically, setting up the bedroom, organising his clothes, putting his phone charger on the bedside table.

His paddle was in his suitcase.

Just in case.

Sarah saw it. "You brought your paddle."

"It doesn't take up much space."

"We agreed. No Padel."

"I know. But what if—"

"Dave. There is no 'what if.' You are not playing Padel in Cornwall."

"The facility in Truro looks really good though."

"Dave."

"They have air conditioning. And a café. And apparently they do coaching sessions—"

"DAVE."

"Fine! I'm not playing Padel in Cornwall!"

But he left the paddle in his suitcase.

Just in case.

The first few days were actually lovely. Beach time. Rock pooling with Emily, who pretended to be too old for it but clearly wasn't. Surfing lessons with Tom, who was surprisingly good. Cream teas. Fish and chips. Long walks along coastal paths while Sarah pointed out birds and Dave pretended to be interested.

He was interested. Mostly. His phone stayed in his pocket. The WhatsApp group stayed unread.

Well. Mostly unread.

He'd checked it a few times. Just to make sure everyone was okay.

Rich, Monday 3:47pm: "Anyone else missing Padel?"

Mike, Monday 4:23pm: "It's been three days. We're fine."

Steve, Monday 5:15pm: "Speak for yourself. I played wall ball in my garage yesterday."

Rich, Monday 5:47pm: "That's quite sad."

Steve, Monday 6:02pm: "It was very sad. I'm very aware."

Mike, Monday 6:34pm: "We all need hobbies for our hobby."

Dave had smiled at that, scrolled through a few more messages, then put his phone away when Sarah gave him that look.

By day five, Dave was getting twitchy.

"You're doing that thing," Sarah observed over breakfast.

"What thing?"

"The fidgety thing. The 'I'm thinking about Padel' thing."

"I'm not thinking about Padel."

"Your leg is bouncing. You check your phone every three minutes. Last night you were watching YouTube in the bathroom."

"That was a documentary about Cornwall."

"It was a Padel tutorial. I saw the thumbnail."

Dave sighed. "Okay. Fine. I'm thinking about Padel a bit."

"A bit?"

"Quite a lot. Possibly constantly."

"Dave. We're on holiday."

"I know. And I'm enjoying it! The beach is great. The cottage is lovely. Yesterday's cream tea was exceptional."

"But?"

"But I miss it. Is that weird?"

"It's very weird."

"It's been five days. That's ten missed sessions. My serve technique—"

"Your serve technique will survive two weeks off."

"Will it though?"

Tom looked up from his toast. "Dad, you're being weird."

"I'm not being weird."

"You're absolutely being weird," Emily agreed. "Yesterday you tried to explain court positioning using rock pools."

"That was educational!"

"That was sad."

Dave looked around the breakfast table. At his family, all staring at him with varying degrees of concern and amusement.

"Fine," he said. "I have a problem. I'm addicted to Padel. There. I said it."

"First step is admitting it," Sarah said.

"What's the second step?"

"Going cold turkey for the rest of the holiday."

"That seems extreme."

"Dave. One session. That's all you want, isn't it? One session to get it out of your system?"

Dave hesitated. This felt like a trap.

"Maybe."

"If I let you play one session, will you promise to be present for the rest of the holiday?"

"You'd let me play?"

"One session. Midweek. You drive to Truro, play for ninety minutes, come back. The rest of the time is family time. Deal?"

Dave looked at Sarah. At the compromise being offered. At his children watching to see what he'd choose.

"Deal," he said.

"Really?" Tom said. "You're actually letting him?"

"Your father needs his fix. Like a smoker. Or a gambler. Or someone with a serious personality disorder."

"I'm right here."

"We know, darling. That's the problem."

Dave booked a court in Truro for Wednesday afternoon. Just a casual pay-and-play session. The facility could match him with other players. Nothing serious. Just ninety minutes of Padel to reset his brain.

Wednesday arrived with sunshine and the kind of anticipation usually reserved for important occasions.

"You're excited," Sarah observed.

"I'm appropriately enthusiastic."

"You've been up since 6am."

"I always wake early on holiday."

"You've checked your paddle three times."

"Just making sure it's still there."

"Where would it go?"

"I don't know. But I needed to check."

The drive to Truro took forty-seven minutes. Dave arrived at the Padel facility - called "Court Side" - with twenty minutes to spare.

It was perfect. Modern. Clean. Six courts, all with proper lighting and air conditioning. A café that sold protein shakes and overpriced granola bars. Everything Dave's Padel-obsessed heart desired.

He checked in. The receptionist assigned him to Court 4. Doubles with three other players. Random pairing.

Dave walked through the facility, paddle in hand, feeling like he'd come home.

Court 4 already had two people warming up. A man in his sixties, grey-haired and lean. A woman about Dave's age, wearing proper Padel gear and looking competent.

"Hi!" Dave said. "I'm Dave. Random booking?"

"Graham," the man said, shaking hands. "And this is Rachel. Welcome. First time at Court Side?"

"First time in Cornwall, actually. On holiday with the family."

Rachel smiled. "And you're spending it playing Padel? Your family must love that."

"My wife's tolerance is significant."

"Same," Graham said. "My wife thinks I'm at a garden centre."

They laughed. The fourth player arrived - a Spanish man called Miguel who was clearly very good and immediately made Dave nervous.

They played. And it was... wonderful. Different court, different players, but the same fundamental joy of hitting a ball and occasionally hitting it where you intended.

Dave's serve was rusty. His positioning was off. But it didn't matter. He was playing Padel. In Cornwall. On holiday. Despite all reasonable objections.

Graham was defensive, patient. Rachel was aggressive, powerful. Miguel was... well, Miguel was Spanish and made them all look like children playing dress-up.

"Where are you from?" Dave asked during a break.

"Seville originally. Here for work. Play three times a week."

"Same! Well, four times actually."

"Four times is good commitment."

"Or obsession. Depending on who you ask."

Miguel smiled. "In Spain, four times is normal. In England, four times is crazy person."

"That's what my wife says."

They played for ninety minutes. Lost both matches but had excellent rallies. Dave's serve came back gradually. His positioning improved. By the end, he felt human again.

In the changing room, exchanging contact details because that's what Padel people did, Graham said: "You're pretty good for a holidaymaker."

"Been playing about six months."

"Shows. You've got proper technique. Coached?"

"Once. Spanish guy called Carlos."

"They're always called Carlos," Rachel laughed.

"Are they?"

"It's apparently a requirement. To coach Padel in England, you must be Spanish and called Carlos."

Dave drove back to St Ives feeling refreshed. Reset. Like he'd scratched an itch that had been building for five days.

Sarah was reading in the garden when he arrived.

"How was it?"

"Good. Really good. Got absolutely demolished by a Spanish guy but it was fun."

"Out of your system?"

Dave thought about this. Was it out of his system? Or had it just made the craving worse?

"Mostly," he lied.

"Good. Because we're having proper family dinner tonight. No phones. No Padel talk. No court positioning demonstrations."

"I can do that."

"Can you though?"

"I'll try very hard."

Dinner was at a seafood restaurant in St Ives. Expensive but lovely. The kind of place where the fish was caught that morning and the menu changed daily.

Tom ordered seabass. Emily ordered mussels. Sarah ordered crab. Dave ordered cod and tried very hard not to check his phone.

"So," Tom said, once the food arrived. "You actually played today."

"I did."

"After five days of withdrawal symptoms."

"I wasn't having withdrawal symptoms."

"Dad, you tried to serve a tennis ball on the beach."

"That was just reflexive."

"You explained the bandeja shot to that family at the cream tea shop."

"They asked!"

"They asked about clotted cream. You made it about Padel."

Sarah laughed despite herself. "He's right. You did do that."

"The family looked terrified," Emily added.

"They looked interested!"

"Dad, they literally ran away."

"They were late for something."

"They were escaping from you."

Dave put down his fork. "Okay. Maybe I have a slight problem."

"Slight?" Tom said.

"Moderate."

"Significant," Sarah corrected.

"Fine. Significant. I have a significant Padel problem."

"But you're happy," Emily said quietly.

Everyone looked at her.

"What?" she continued. "He is. I haven't seen Dad this enthusiastic about anything in years. Maybe ever."

"That's not true," Dave protested. "I was enthusiastic a bout... things."

"Name one."

"Work?"

"You hate your job."

"I don't hate it. It's fine."

"You call it 'soul-destroying' every Sunday evening."

This was unfortunately accurate.

"Okay but I'm enthusiastic about... family?"

"That's obligatory," Tom said.

"Not obligatory. Genuine!"

"But you're not excited about it," Emily said. "Not like you are about Padel. When you talk about Padel, your whole face changes. You get animated. You care."

Dave looked at Sarah, who was watching him with an unreadable expression.

"She's right," Sarah said. "You do care. About this ridiculous sport and your ridiculous friends and your ridiculous spreadsheets. And that's... that's actually nice to see."

"Really?"

"Really. As long as you don't forget about us completely."

"I won't."

"Promise?"

"Promise. No more rock pool court positioning. No more Padel talk at cream tea shops. Just family time. Well. Mostly family time."

"We'll take mostly," Tom said.

They finished dinner. Walked along the harbour. Watched the sunset over St Ives Bay. Dave's phone stayed in his pocket. The WhatsApp group stayed unread.

Mostly.

He checked it once. Just before bed. While Sarah was brushing her teeth.

Rich, Wednesday 8:47pm: "Dave's been quiet. Think he's okay?"

Mike, Wednesday 9:02pm: "Probably playing Padel somewhere."

Steve, Wednesday 9:15pm: "No way. Sarah wouldn't let him."

Rich, Wednesday 9:23pm: "£10 says he found a court."

Mike, Wednesday 9:34pm: "£10 says he's tried to build a court on the beach."

Steve, Wednesday 9:47pm: "£10 says he's explaining Padel to confused tourists."

Dave smiled, typed a reply.

Dave, Wednesday 10:52pm: "Played this afternoon. It was excellent. Wife's tolerance confirmed as extraordinary."

Rich, Wednesday 10:53pm: "KNEW IT."

Mike, Wednesday 10:54pm: "You owe me £10."

Steve, Wednesday 10:55pm: "How was it really?"

Dave, Wednesday 10:57pm: "Good. Different players. Spanish guy destroyed us. But good."

Rich, Wednesday 10:59pm: "There's always a Spanish guy."

Mike, Wednesday 11:02pm: "It's mandatory apparently."

Dave, Wednesday 11:04pm: "Right. Signing off. Promised actual family time for rest of holiday."

Steve, Wednesday 11:06pm: "Respect."

Rich, Wednesday 11:07pm: "See you when you're back. We're joint eighth now."

Dave, Wednesday 11:08pm: "JOINT EIGHTH?!"

Mike, Wednesday 11:09pm: "Won both matches last Saturday. Miracle occurred."

Dave, Wednesday 11:11pm: "HOW DID I MISS THIS?!"

Rich, Wednesday 11:12pm: "You were on holiday. Like a normal person."

Dave, Wednesday 11:14pm: "Need full breakdown. Stats. Analysis. Everything."

Mike, Wednesday 11:15pm: "Tomorrow. Go spend time with your family."

Dave, Wednesday 11:16pm: "But—"

Steve, Wednesday 11:17pm: "FAMILY TIME, DAVE."

Dave, Wednesday 11:18pm: "Fine. But first thing Monday morning, full debrief."

Rich, Wednesday 11:19pm: "Deal."

Dave put his phone down. Sarah emerged from the bathroom.

"Checking Padel messages?"

"Maybe."

"How are the boys?"

"They won both matches last Saturday. We're joint eighth."

"That's good?"

"That's amazing! We were joint tenth! That's two places!"

"Dave. It's 11pm. You're on holiday. And you're excited about other people's Padel matches."

"I know. It's weird."

"It's very weird."

"But also kind of nice?"

Sarah climbed into bed. "It is nice. You caring about something. Having friends. Being part of something. Just... try to remember there's life outside the glass cage, yeah?"

"I know."

"Do you though?"

Dave thought about Cornwall. About the beach and the cream teas and the family dinners. About Tom and Emily and Sarah and proper holidays that didn't involve Padel.

About the ninety minutes that afternoon that had made him feel complete again.

"I'm trying," he said.

"That's all I ask."

They lay in the dark, listening to waves in the distance and seagulls making their final evening complaints.

"One more question," Sarah said.

"Yeah?"

"When we get back, are you going to immediately book more courts?"

Dave hesitated. Considered lying.

"Probably," he admitted.

"At midnight?"

"Most likely."

"While I'm sleeping next to you?"

"Almost certainly."

Sarah sighed. The kind of sigh that contained love and exasperation and acceptance in equal measure.

"At least you're honest."

"It's one of my few remaining qualities."

"You have other qualities."

"Name one."

"You're... enthusiastic."

"About Padel."

"About something. That's more than most people."

Dave rolled over, kissed her forehead. "Thank you for letting me play today."

"Thank you for being present the rest of the time."

"Mostly present."

"Mostly present counts."

They fell asleep to the sound of waves and seagulls and Dave's phone buzzing occasionally with WhatsApp messages that could wait until morning.

Probably.

Maybe.

He checked them at 6:47am.

Obviously.

There were seventeen new messages. Mostly about strategy for the next league matches. Some about equipment. One from Steve about whether anyone wanted to watch professional Padel on YouTube together.

Dave replied to all of them while making coffee.

Sarah found him at the kitchen table, phone in hand, coffee going cold, completely absorbed in Padel discussions.

"And we're back," she said.

"Sorry. Just catching up."

"It's been eight hours."

"A lot can happen in eight hours."

"In a WhatsApp group about Padel?"

"You'd be surprised."

Sarah poured herself coffee. Sat down. Looked at him with that expression he knew so well.

"You're impossible."

"I know."

"This obsession is ridiculous."

"I know."

"But you're happy."

"I really am."

"Then I suppose that's what matters."

"Even though it's ridiculous?"

"Especially because it's ridiculous."

They sat in the Cornwall morning, Dave's phone still buzzing with messages, Sarah's coffee still steaming, the holiday still ongoing.

Just with slightly more Padel than originally planned.

But that was okay.

That was life now.

And life, against all odds, was pretty bloody good.

Even in Cornwall.

Especially in Cornwall, actually.

Because Dave had found a court.

And that made everything worthwhile.

Probably.

Chapter Eleven
The Rival Match

By September, The Rookies had developed something that could generously be called a rivalry.

The team was called "Court Jesters." They were roughly the same level of terrible. They'd entered the league with similar enthusiasm and similar delusions about their abilities. And over the course of fourteen weeks, they'd played each other four times.

The record stood at 2-2.

"This is it," Rich said at training on the Thursday before their fifth and final match. "The decider."

"It's not really a decider," Steve pointed out. "We're seventh. They're eighth. Neither of us are making the finals."

"It's a psychological decider."

"That's not a thing."

"It absolutely is. Winner gets bragging rights for the entire off-season."

"What off-season?" Mike asked. "We're playing year-round now."

"Exactly. So bragging rights are permanent."

Dave had been tracking the Court Jesters all season. Not obsessively. Just... comprehensively. He had a separate spreadsheet tab dedicated to their performance. Their strengths. Their weaknesses. Their tendencies in pressure situations.

"This is excessive," Sarah had said when she'd seen it.

"This is preparation."

"Dave. It's a spreadsheet about your rivals' serving patterns."

"Their left-side player serves wide 73% of the time. That's actionable intelligence."

"That's stalker behaviour."

"It's sports analysis."

The WhatsApp group had been buzzing all week.

Rich, Monday 9:47am: "Saturday is huge."

Mike, Monday 10:23am: "It's really not that huge."

Rich, Monday 10:34am: "2-2 record. Final match. Winner takes the season series. That's objectively huge."

Steve, Monday 11:15am: "Winner takes literally nothing except the knowledge they're slightly less terrible than the other team."

Rich, Monday 11:28am: "EXACTLY. That knowledge is everything."

Dave, Monday 2:47pm: "I've been analyzing their game footage."

Mike, Monday 2:53pm: "There's game footage?"

Dave, Monday 2:55pm: "Someone's been recording matches. Posted them on YouTube."

Steve, Monday 3:12pm: "You found game footage of Court Jesters?"

Dave, Monday 3:15pm: "I found game footage of us too. From week 6. It's... humbling."

Rich, Monday 3:24pm: "How bad?"

Dave, Monday 3:26pm: "We were terrible. But so were they. That's comforting."

Mike, Monday 3:38pm: "Send links?"

Dave sent the links. By Tuesday evening, they'd all watched every available video multiple times. Dave had made notes. Rich had created a PowerPoint presentation. Mike had drawn diagrams on his whiteboard at school and his students had asked if he was okay.

Steve had done none of these things but had definitely watched the videos.

"This is mental," he'd messaged privately to Dave.

"Which part?"

"All of it. The videos. The analysis. Rich's PowerPoint has forty-seven slides."

"I know. It's very thorough."

"It's very insane."

"Same thing really."

Thursday's training session was intense. They practiced serving patterns. Return techniques. Court positioning. Communication. Everything that might give them an edge.

"Remember," Rich said during a break, "they always poach on the third shot. We can exploit that."

"How?" Mike asked.

"By hitting the fourth shot down the line."

"What if we don't get to the fourth shot?"

"Then we improve our third shot."

"That's circular logic."

"That's Padel."

By the end of the session, they'd drilled every scenario Dave's spreadsheet had identified. They'd practiced their serves until Mike's shoulder hurt. They'd done court positioning exercises until Steve threatened to leave.

"We're ready," Rich declared.

"We're overtrained," Steve countered.

"Is there such a thing?"

"We're about to find out."

Friday evening, Dave couldn't sleep. Kept thinking about the match. About the 2-2 record. About their rival team who were basically them but slightly different.

Sarah found him in the kitchen at 11:47pm, staring at his phone.

"You're not watching Padel videos."

"I'm not watching Padel videos."

"Dave."

"Fine. I'm watching Padel videos."

"It's midnight."

"Technically it's eleven forty-seven."

"What are you watching?"

"Our game from week 6. Looking for patterns."

Sarah sat down next to him. "Dave. You've done everything you can. You've prepared. You've analyzed. You've created spreadsheets and watched videos and driven your friends slightly mad. Now you just need to play."

"But what if we lose?"

"Then you lose. And the world continues. And you're still seventh in the league. And everything is exactly the same except you've lost to Court Jesters."

"But they'll have bragging rights."

"Do you even interact with them outside of matches?"

"No. But I'll know. We'll all know."

Sarah took his phone, put it face down on the table. "Dave. Listen to me. This is supposed to be fun."

"It is fun."

"Is it? Really? Because you look stressed. You haven't slept properly all week. You're watching match footage at midnight like it's the World Cup final."

"It's important."

"It's a hobby."

"It's our hobby. That's what makes it important."

Sarah was quiet for a moment. "Okay. I get that. But promise me something."

"What?"

"Tomorrow, after the match, win or lose, you'll remember that you're playing a sport in a glass cage with your mates. Not trying to cure cancer or solve world peace. Just... hitting a ball."

"Just hitting a ball," Dave repeated.

"Just hitting a ball."

"Okay. I can do that."

"Can you though?"

"I'll try very hard."

Saturday morning arrived with the kind of nervous energy usually reserved for job interviews or surgery.

Dave was at ActiveLife forty-five minutes early. So was Mike. Then Steve. Then Rich.

"We're all here early," Mike observed.

"Apparently it's important," Steve said.

"It's very important," Rich corrected.

Court Jesters arrived looking similarly nervous. They nodded at each other. The kind of respectful nod that acknowledged they were about to go to war but could be civil about it.

Their captain - a man called Derek who worked in insurance - approached Dave.

"Big match," he said.

"2-2 record. Makes it interesting."

"My team's been practicing all week."

"Same."

"May the best terrible team win."

"Agreed."

They shook hands. Took their positions.

The first match was Dave and Rich against Derek and his partner Martin.

Rich served first. Good serve. Into the corner. Derek returned it. Dave positioned himself, saw the ball coming, swung—

Perfect contact. Right down the middle. Martin tried to return it, hit the net.

1-0.

"YES!" Mike shouted from the bench.

They'd scored first. That felt significant. That felt like momentum.

The game continued. They were focused. Communicating. Moving well. Every drill they'd practiced, every pattern they'd identified, every strategy session—it was all coming together.

They won the first game 11-7.

Mike and Steve high-fived them as they came off. "That was brilliant! Keep it going!"

Second match was Mike and Steve against Court Jesters' other pair.

They lost 11-8. Close. Competitive. But lost.

1-1.

Everything rested on the third game. Dave and Rich again.

"Pressure's on," Rich said, bouncing on his toes.

"No pressure," Dave lied. "Just another game."

They took the court. The atmosphere had changed. Everyone watching knew this was the decider. Joint seventh vs joint eighth. Pride on the line. Bragging rights for the entire off-season.

Dave served. His hand was shaking slightly. The ball went over but with no power.

Easy return. Rich hit it back. Rally started. Five shots. Six. Seven.

Derek hit it wide.

1-0.

They played point by point. Game went to 3-3. Then 5-5. Then 7-7.

Every point was a battle. Every rally lasted forever. Dave's legs were burning. His elbow was complaining. But he kept moving. Kept competing.

9-9.

Two points to win.

Court Jesters served. Dave returned it. Rally started. Rich hit a good shot to the corner. Martin retrieved it. Dave positioned himself. Saw the opportunity. Hit the bandeja.

The shot Carlos had taught them. The one they'd practiced hundreds of times. The one Dave had only successfully executed in matches about three times.

The ball bounced awkwardly off the back glass. Derek tried to return it. Missed.

10-9.

Match point.

Dave's turn to serve. His heart was hammering. This was it. This was everything.

He bounced the ball. Once. Twice. Three times.

Served.

Good serve. Deep. Into the corner.

Derek returned it. High and floating.

Rich moved forward. Positioned himself. Hit a perfect volley. Down the line. Unreturnable.

Point.

Game.

Match.

The Rookies exploded. Literally jumped and shouted and hugged each other like they'd won an actual championship.

Court Jesters looked disappointed but came to shake hands.

"Good match," Derek said.

"Really good match," Dave agreed, still breathing hard.

"See you next season?"

"Definitely."

They gathered their stuff. Walked to the changing room. Couldn't stop grinning.

"We won," Mike kept saying. "We actually won."

"3-2 season record," Rich said. "Winners of the series."

"Joint seventh in the league," Steve added.

"With a winning record against our rivals," Dave finished.

They sat in the changing room, still in their sweaty kit, not quite ready to move.

"That was the best match we've played," Rich said quietly.

"By far," Mike agreed.

"We actually looked competent," Steve said.

"We looked like we knew what we were doing."

"We looked like a team."

Dave's phone was buzzing. He pulled it out. Sarah had texted.

"How did it go?"

Dave typed: "We won. 3-2. Season series victory."

Three dots appeared.

"Well done. I'm proud of you for caring about something this much x"

Dave stared at the message. Sarah understood. She'd been skeptical, mocking, exasperated. But she understood.

He showed the message to the others.

"That's nice," Mike said.

"Very supportive," Rich agreed.

"My ex-wife would have said 'cool' and changed the subject," Steve said.

"Is that why she's your ex-wife?"

"One of many reasons."

They changed. Gathered their stuff. Walked out to the car park still buzzing with adrenaline and achievement.

"Pub?" Rich suggested.

"Absolutely," Mike said immediately.

"I could drink," Steve agreed.

"Dave?" Rich looked at him.

Dave checked the time. 11:47am. He was supposed to help Sarah with food shopping. They'd planned lunch together.

"One pint," he said. "Then I need to get home."

"One pint," Rich agreed.

It was not one pint.

It was three pints and several bags of crisps and approximately two hours of reliving every single point of the match.

Dave texted Sarah at 1:30pm: "Still at pub. Sorry. Won the match. Celebrating. Home by 3?"

Sarah replied: "Take your time. You earned it. But you're doing dinner tonight x"

At 2:45pm, Dave's phone rang. It was Tom.

"Dad?"

"Tom! Hi! We won! Beat Court Jesters 3-2! Season series victory!"

"That's... great, Dad. Um. Where are you?"

"Pub. With the lads. Celebrating."

"Right. Mum sent me to check you're okay."

"I'm perfect! We won! Did I mention we won?"

"Several times. How much have you had to drink?"

"Three pints. Maybe four. Lost count."

"Dad. It's 2pm on a Saturday."

"Victory doesn't operate on a schedule!"

Tom laughed. "Okay. Fair enough. Just... get home safely, yeah?"

"Will do. Love you!"

"Love you too, Dad. Congratulations."

Dave hung up. Looked at his three friends, all slightly drunk, all grinning like idiots.

"My son thinks I'm drunk."

"You are drunk," Steve said.

"On victory!"

"And beer."

"Mostly beer actually."

"Should we get another round?"

"Absolutely."

They didn't get another round. Rich's wife called and reminded him they had dinner plans. Mike realized he'd promised Clare he'd mow the lawn. Steve had a job to quote that afternoon.

Dave drove home very carefully, windows down, singing along to Radio 2, feeling like he'd accomplished something significant.

Sarah was in the garden when he arrived.

"You're drunk," she observed.

"I'm happy."

"You're drunk and happy."

"We won."

"I know. You texted me. And called me. And sent me a video of the final point."

"Did you watch it?"

"I watched it. Very dramatic."

"Right?!"

"Dave. You need to eat something and drink water."

"I need to tell you about the match."

"I'm sure you do."

Dave launched into a point-by-point breakdown of the entire match. Sarah listened patiently, occasionally nodding, making appropriate noises.

"That sounds excellent," she said when he finished.

"It was! We were a team! An actual functioning team!"

"I'm proud of you."

"Really?"

"Really. You worked hard. You prepared. You cared. And you won. That's something."

"It's joint seventh."

"It's progress."

Dave hugged her. She tolerated it despite him being sweaty and slightly drunk and smelling of pub.

"Thank you," he said.

"For what?"

"For understanding. For letting me be ridiculous. For not leaving me despite the midnight bookings and the spreadsheets and the general obsession."

"You're welcome. Now go shower. You smell terrible."

That evening, Dave made dinner as promised. Pasta. Slightly overcooked because he was still drunk and distracted, but edible.

They ate together, the four of them. Tom and Emily asking about the match. Dave explaining with only slightly less enthusiasm than earlier. Sarah watching him talk, seeing him animated and happy and present.

"You're different," Emily said eventually.

"Different how?"

"Just... lighter. Like you're actually enjoying life instead of just going through it."

Dave thought about this. About the past nine months. About finding Padel and finding friends and finding something that made him set midnight alarms and create forty-eight-tab spreadsheets and generally lose his mind.

"I think I am," he said. "Enjoying life, I mean."

"Because of Padel?" Tom asked.

"Because of... everything. Padel. The lads. Having something to work toward. Feeling part of something."

"That's nice, Dad," Emily said.

"It is nice. It's very nice."

Later, in bed, Sarah asked: "Was it worth it?"

"What?"

"All of it. The obsession. The time. The money. The spreadsheets. Was today's victory worth all that?"

Dave thought about the match. About the final point. About Rich's perfect volley and the celebration and the pub and coming home drunk at 3pm on a Saturday.

About nine months of training and midnight bookings and YouTube videos and equipment purchases and injuries and analysis and dedication.

About Court Jesters and their 2-2 record that became 3-2.

"Yeah," he said. "Absolutely worth it."

"Even though it's just a hobby?"

"Even though it's just a hobby."

"Even though you're still joint seventh?"

"Even though we're still joint seventh."

Sarah was quiet for a moment. "You're completely mad."

"I know."

"This whole thing is ridiculous."

"I know."

"But you're happy."

"I really am."

"Then I suppose that's all that matters."

Dave's phone buzzed. WhatsApp. The group reliving the match. Again. For the fourteenth time.

Rich, 10:47pm: "Still can't believe that final point."

Mike, 10:52pm: "Dave's serve was perfect."

Steve, 10:58pm: "Rich's volley though. Chef's kiss."

Dave, 11:03pm: "We were all brilliant. Team effort."

Rich, 11:07pm: "Season series winners."

Mike, 11:11pm: "Never gets old saying that."

Steve, 11:15pm: "Still joint seventh though."

Rich, 11:18pm: "Still counts."

Dave, 11:21pm: "Three matches left. If we win all three..."

Mike, 11:24pm: "We could be joint sixth?"

Rich, 11:27pm: "Aim high."

Steve, 11:30pm: "Aim realistic."

Dave, 11:33pm: "Where's the fun in that?"

Sarah reached over, took his phone, put it on her bedside table.

"Sleep," she said.

"Just finishing—"

"Dave. Sleep."

"But we're discussing next week's matches."

"Discuss them tomorrow."

"Fine."

Dave closed his eyes. Thought about victory and rivalry and friendship and purpose.

About Court Jesters and their disappointed faces and the respectful handshake afterwards.

About being joint seventh and having a winning season series and caring about things that didn't matter except they did.

He fell asleep smiling.

Dreaming about Padel.

Obviously.

But happy dreams this time.

Victory dreams.

Season series winner dreams.

Joint seventh dreams.

Which were, it turned out, the best kind of dreams.

Probably.

Chapter Twelve
The Reality Check

It started with Dave missing Tom's university presentation.

Not intentionally. He'd had it in his calendar. "Tom's Architecture Presentation - 6pm." He'd set a reminder. Two reminders, actually. He'd fully intended to be there.

But there was a Thursday evening training session at 7pm. And Thursday traffic was bad. And if he went to Tom's presentation at 6pm, he'd never make training by 7pm.

And they had an important league match on Saturday.

And the logical thing - the only logical thing - was to skip the presentation and go to training.

Tom would understand.

Tom didn't understand.

"You promised," he said on the phone that evening.

Dave was in his car, driving to ActiveLife. "I know. I'm sorry. Traffic was terrible and I just couldn't make both—"

"You chose Padel over my presentation."

"It's not like that."

"What's it like then?"

"It's... complicated. We've got a match on Saturday. We need to practice. The team—"

"The team. Right. Your Padel team is more important than your son."

"That's not what I'm saying."

"That's exactly what you're saying."

The line went dead. Tom had hung up.

Dave sat in the ActiveLife car park, engine still running, phone in his hand.

He could turn around. Drive home. Call Tom. Apologize properly. Miss training.

Or he could go in. Play. Apologize to Tom tomorrow when emotions weren't so high.

He went in.

The training session was good. They worked on serves. Practiced returns. Did positioning drills. Everything they needed for Saturday.

But Dave's mind wasn't fully present. Kept thinking about Tom. About the phone call. About "you chose Padel over my son."

"You alright?" Steve asked during a break.

"Fine."

"You're playing like someone who's not fine."

"Just... family stuff."

"Want to talk about it?"

"Not really."

They played on. Dave tried to focus. Tried to be present. Kept missing shots he should have made.

At home, Tom was in his room. Door closed. Music on.

The universal sign of teenage - well, twenty-year-old - sulking.

Sarah was in the kitchen, very carefully not looking at Dave.

"I messed up," Dave said.

"You did."

"I should have gone to his presentation."

"You should have."

"I'll apologize tomorrow."

"Will you though? Or will there be another training session or match or midnight booking that's somehow more important?"

"That's not fair."

Sarah put down the knife she'd been using to chop vegetables. "Dave. When was the last time you were present for something that wasn't Padel-related?"

"I'm present lots!"

"When?"

Dave thought hard. "Dinner. We had dinner together on Sunday."

"After you came back from training."

"Well, yes, but—"

"And you spent half of it explaining court positioning to Emily."

"She was interested!"

"She was being polite."

Dave sat down heavily at the kitchen table. "Okay. Maybe I've been a bit... absent."

"A bit?"

"Quite absent."

"Very absent. Extremely absent. You're physically here but mentally you're always in a glass cage hitting a ball."

"That's dramatic."

"Is it? Tom's presentation was important to him. He'd been working on it for weeks. He specifically asked you to be there. And you chose Padel."

"I didn't choose—" Dave stopped. Thought about it. About the decision in the car. About driving to ActiveLife instead of driving home. "Okay. I chose Padel."

"And that's the problem. You're always choosing Padel. Over family. Over work. Over everything."

"Work's fine. I've never missed a deadline."

"You're distracted constantly. Priya told me you've been in three meetings this month where you zoned out completely."

"Priya told you?"

"We ran into each other at Tesco. She was concerned. Said you seem 'elsewhere' lately."

Dave couldn't argue. He had been elsewhere. Had been thinking about serves during meetings. About court positioning during presentations. About league standings during budget reviews.

"I'll fix it," he said.

"How?"

"I'll... be more present. Focus more. Balance things better."

"Dave. You're playing four times a week. Watching videos every night. Setting midnight alarms. Creating spreadsheets with fifty-three tabs now, apparently. When exactly are you going to find time to balance things?"

"I'll cut back."

"Will you though?"

Dave thought about cutting back. About missing sessions. About letting the team down. About falling behind in the league.

"Maybe," he said weakly.

Sarah's expression softened slightly. "Dave. I'm not asking you to quit. I know it makes you happy. I know it's important to you. But it can't be the only thing that's important to you."

"It's not."

"Then prove it. Talk to Tom. Actually talk to him. Be present. Not just physically there but actually engaged."

"I will."

"And maybe... maybe skip one session a week. Just one. Use that time for family stuff."

Dave felt a spike of panic. Skip a session? Which one? They all mattered. Wednesday was technique work. Thursday was tactical. Saturday was league. Sunday was endurance training.

"I'll think about it," he said.

"That means no."

"It means I'll think about it."

Sarah went back to chopping vegetables. "Your son is upstairs feeling like he's less important than a hobby. You need to fix that. Actually fix it. Not just apologize and then carry on exactly the same."

That night, Dave knocked on Tom's door.

"Go away."

"Tom. Can we talk?"

"Nothing to talk about."

"Please."

Silence. Then: "Fine. Come in."

Tom was at his desk, laptop open, architecture drawings spread around him. The presentation Dave had missed.

"These look amazing," Dave said, meaning it.

"You didn't see them."

"I'm seeing them now."

"It's not the same."

Dave sat on Tom's bed. "You're right. It's not. And I'm sorry. I should have been there."

"But you had Padel."

"That's not an excuse."

"It's the reason though."

Dave couldn't argue. "I messed up. I've been messing up a lot lately."

"You've been obsessed."

"I know."

"Like, properly obsessed. It's all you talk about. All you think about. Mum says you dream about it."

"Occasionally."

"Dad. You sleep-talked about serving technique last week."

"Oh."

"Yeah. 'Oh.' This has gotten out of hand."

Dave looked at his son. Twenty years old. Studying architecture. Brilliant and talented and completely right about everything.

"When did you get so sensible?" Dave asked.

"Someone had to be."

"Fair point."

They sat in silence for a moment.

"I am sorry," Dave said. "Really sorry. Not just for missing the presentation. For being absent. For being obsessed. For choosing Padel over... well, everything."

"Are you going to change?"

"I'm going to try."

"That's what people say when they're not going to change."

"Tom—"

"Dad. I get it. You've found something you love. Something that makes you happy. That's great. Really. But you've got to find balance. Otherwise you're going to wake up one day and realize you've missed everything that actually matters."

"You matter."

"Do I? More than Padel?"

Dave hesitated. Just for a second. Just the briefest pause.

It was enough.

"Right," Tom said, turning back to his laptop. "That's what I thought."

"Tom, that's not— I didn't mean— You're more important than Padel. Obviously you are."

"You hesitated."

"I was thinking about how to phrase it."

"You were deciding if it was true."

Dave wanted to argue. Wanted to insist that of course Tom was more important. That family was always more important. That Padel was just a hobby.

But the hesitation had told the truth.

In that moment, asked to choose, Dave had actually had to think about it.

"I'll do better," Dave said quietly.

"Okay."

"I mean it."

"Okay."

"Tom—"

"Dad. I believe you believe that. But I also know you. You'll try for a week. Maybe two. Then there'll be an important match or a training session you can't miss or some crisis with the lads. And you'll be right back to choosing Padel over everything else."

"That's not fair."

"Isn't it?"

Dave left Tom's room feeling worse than when he'd entered.

The WhatsApp group was buzzing. Discussion about Saturday's match. Strategy. Analysis. Someone had posted a video of professional Padel players demonstrating technique.

Dave watched the video. Made notes. Replied to messages.

Realized he was doing exactly what Tom had said he'd do.

He put his phone down.

Picked it up again thirty seconds later.

The video was really informative.

At work the next day, Priya found him in the kitchen.

"Sarah mentioned she ran into you," Dave said.

"She did. She's worried about you."

"I'm fine."

"Are you? Because you've been distracted for months. The team's noticed."

"The team?"

"Dave. You zoned out in the budget meeting last week. Trevor had to ask you the same question three times."

"I was thinking about something."

"About Padel?"

"Maybe."

"Dave. Listen. I'm saying this as a friend. You need to sort this out. Your work is suffering. Your family is suffering. You're suffering, even if you don't realize it."

"I'm not suffering. I'm happy."

"Are you? Really? Because you look stressed. You look exhausted. You look like someone who's running themselves into the ground trying to be good at something that ultimately doesn't matter."

"It matters to me."

"Does it matter more than your job? More than your family? More than your health?"

Dave didn't answer.

"That hesitation," Priya said gently, "is your answer."

The league match on Saturday was against "The Base-line Bandits." A good team. Significantly better than The Rookies.

They lost 3-0.

Badly.

Dave played terribly. Distracted. Unfocused. Thinking about Tom and Sarah and Priya and all the ways he was apparently failing at life.

"You okay?" Rich asked afterwards.

"Fine."

"You played like someone who wasn't fine."

"Just an off day."

"Dave. Mate. What's going on?"

Dave sat in the changing room, still in his sweaty kit, feeling the weight of everything.

"I missed my son's presentation on Thursday," he said. "Chose training over him. He's barely speaking to me."

Rich was quiet for a moment. "That's rough."

"Sarah says I'm always choosing Padel over everything else."

"Are you?"

"Apparently."

Mike and Steve had been listening. Now they gathered round.

"Family's important," Mike said. "More important than this."

"I know that."

"Do you though?" Steve asked. "Because from where I'm sitting, you're pretty all-in on Padel."

"We all are."

"Yeah, but we're single or our wives have given up caring or we don't have kids who need us anymore. You've got Tom and Emily and Sarah. And you're choosing to be here instead of with them."

"It's not that simple."

"Isn't it?"

They sat in silence. Four middle-aged men in a changing room, confronting uncomfortable truths.

"What are you going to do?" Rich asked eventually.

"I don't know. Sarah suggested cutting back to three sessions a week."

"That's reasonable."

"Is it? Which session do I skip? They're all important."

"Dave. Listen to yourself. You're arguing that four weekly Padel sessions are all essential. That's not normal behaviour."

"Since when do we care about normal?"

"Since your family is suffering."

Dave knew they were right. Knew he'd crossed a line somewhere. Knew he needed to fix this.

"I'll cut back," he said. "One session. Maybe Thursday."

"Why not Sunday?" Mike suggested.

"Sunday is endurance training."

"Dave—"

"Fine. Thursday. I'll skip Thursday."

"Starting when?"

"Next week."

"This week," Rich said firmly. "Start this week. Go home. Spend time with your family. Miss Thursday's session."

"But—"

"Dave. Your son is more important than court positioning drills."

"I know that."

"Then act like it."

Dave drove home in silence. Radio off. Phone in his pocket, buzzing with WhatsApp notifications he didn't check.

Sarah was in the garden, reading.

"How did it go?"

"We lost. Three-nil."

"Sorry."

"It's fine. We were outmatched." Dave sat down next to her. "I'm skipping Thursday sessions. Starting this week."

Sarah looked up from her book. "Really?"

"Really. You're right. Tom's right. Everyone's right. I've been obsessed. I've been absent. I've been choosing Padel over the things that actually matter."

"Dave—"

"No. It's true. And I'm going to fix it. One less session per week. More family time. More present. I promise."

Sarah studied him. "You're sure?"

"I'm sure. Well. I'm trying to be sure. It's... harder than it should be. Which is its own problem."

"It's a start though."

"It's a start."

That evening, Dave texted the group.

Dave, 6:47pm: "Need to skip Thursdays from now on. Family commitments."

Rich, 6:52pm: "Completely understand."

Mike, 6:54pm: "Makes sense. We'll miss you but we'll manage."

Steve, 7:01pm: "Good for you. Seriously. Prioritizing what matters."

Dave, 7:05pm: "Thanks. Still doing Wed, Sat, Sun."

Rich, 7:08pm: "That's plenty. More than most people."

Mike, 7:11pm: "Three times a week is still proper commitment."

Steve, 7:15pm: "Three times a week is still probably too much."

Dave, 7:18pm: "Baby steps."

He knocked on Tom's door.

"Yeah?"

"Can I show you the architecture drawings properly? You can explain them to me. I'll actually listen this time."

Tom hesitated. Then: "Okay. Come in."

They spent an hour going through Tom's presentation. Dave asked questions. Actually listened to the answers. Didn't check his phone once.

Well. Once. But very briefly. And he put it away immediately when Tom gave him a look.

"This is really impressive," Dave said, meaning it.

"Thanks."

"I'm proud of you."

"Thanks, Dad."

"And I'm sorry. For missing it. For being absent. For being obsessed with something stupid when I should have been focused on you."

"Padel's not stupid."

"It's quite stupid."

"Yeah, but it makes you happy. That's not stupid."

"Even if I've been neglecting everything else for it?"

"You're fixing that now though. Right?"

"I'm trying to."

"That's all I'm asking."

They sat in Tom's room, surrounded by architecture drawings and laptop screens and evidence of Tom's talent.

"I missed a lot, didn't I?" Dave said.

"A bit."

"More than a bit."

"Yeah. More than a bit."

"I'll do better."

"I know. Just... actually do better. Don't just say it."

"Deal."

Later, in bed, Sarah asked: "How do you feel?"

"Guilty. Ashamed. Like I've been an idiot."

"You have been an idiot."

"Thanks."

"But you're fixing it. That's what matters."

"Three sessions a week still feels like a lot."

"It is a lot. But it's better than four."

"Baby steps."

"Baby steps."

Dave's phone buzzed. WhatsApp. He ignored it.

It buzzed again.

And again.

"You can check it," Sarah said.

"I'm being present."

"Dave. Check your phone. Just don't disappear into it."

Dave checked. The group was discussing Wednesday's session. Strategy for next week's match. Someone had posted another video.

He read the messages. Didn't reply. Put the phone down.

"See?" he said. "Present."

"Very impressive."

"I'm working on it."

"I can see that."

They lay in the dark, Sarah's breathing evening out as she fell asleep.

Dave's phone buzzed again.

He didn't check it.

Well. He checked it at 6:47am the next morning.

Obviously.

But he'd made it through the night.

Baby steps.

Progress.

Balance.

Probably.

Chapter Thirteen
The Tournament

The email arrived in early November.

"ActiveLife Winter Doubles Tournament - December 21st"

Dave saw it at 7:23am while having breakfast. By 7:24am he'd read it three times. By 7:25am he'd forwarded it to the group.

Dave, 7:26am: "Winter tournament. December 21st. Doubles. We're entering, right?"

Rich, 7:31am: "Obviously."

Mike, 7:34am: "Obviously."

Steve, 7:38am: "Do we have to?"

Rich, 7:40am: "Yes."

Steve, 7:42am: "But we're terrible."

Mike, 7:44am: "We're less terrible than we used to be."

Dave, 7:46am: "We're joint sixth now."

Steve, 7:48am: "Out of twelve teams. That's exactly middle. That's the definition of mediocre."

Rich, 7:50am: "Mediocre is generous. But we've improved."

Dave, 7:52am: "We've won five matches total."

Mike, 7:54am: "That's five more than zero."

Steve, 7:56am: "Hard to argue with that logic."

By 8am they'd all entered. Dave and Rich as one pair. Mike and Steve as another.

"Tournament," Sarah said when Dave told her over dinner. "Is that like league?"

"It's a one-day knockout competition. Proper tournament format."

"And you're entering despite being, what did you say, joint sixth?"

"Joint sixth with an improving trajectory."

"That's not a thing."

"It absolutely is. We've won three of our last five matches."

"So you've lost two."

"But won three! That's 60% win rate!"

"Dave. Listen to yourself."

"What?"

"You're celebrating a 60% win rate in the beginners' league of a sport you've been doing for ten months."

"It's progress!"

"It's madness."

"Can't it be both?"

Sarah smiled despite herself. "I suppose it can."

The tournament was five weeks away. Which meant five weeks of preparation. Five weeks of training. Five weeks of Dave creating increasingly complex spreadsheets.

"What's this one?" Sarah asked, finding him at the laptop late one evening.

"Tournament bracket projection."

"There isn't a bracket yet."

"But there will be. And I want to be prepared for all possible matchups."

"Dave. You can't prepare for something that doesn't exist."

"That's quitter talk."

He'd created a spreadsheet with every possible tournament scenario. Who they might play in round one. Round two. Potential quarter-finals. Semi-finals. Finals.

"This assumes we win every match," Sarah pointed out.

"It's aspirational."

"It's delusional."

"Same thing really."

The tournament preparation took over everything. Wednesday sessions became focused drilling. Saturday matches became tournament simulation. Sunday sessions became endurance training.

Dave had stuck to his promise about skipping Thursdays. Mostly. He'd only suggested training "just this once" twice. And only actually done it once. Which was progress.

Probably.

"How's the balance going?" Tom asked one evening.

"Good! I skipped Thursday training for three weeks straight."

"And the fourth week?"

"Had to practice. Important match on Saturday."

"Dad."

"What? Three out of four is 75%! That's a solid B!"

"That's not how it works."

"Isn't it though?"

Tom sighed the sigh of someone who'd inherited his father's stubbornness and was now forced to witness it.

"Just... try to remember the tournament isn't actually important."

"It's very important."

"In what way?"

"It's... a test. Of progress. Of improvement. Of whether we've actually gotten better or just gotten used to being terrible."

"And if you lose?"

"Then we've learned something."

"What will you have learned?"

"That we're still terrible. But less terrible than we were. Which is its own kind of victory."

"You've got an answer for everything."

"Years of practice."

The WhatsApp group was in constant motion. Strategy discussions. Technique videos. Motivational messages at inappropriate times.

Rich, 11:47pm: "Five weeks until tournament. That's fifteen sessions. Make each one count."

Mike, 11:52pm: "It's midnight."

Rich, 11:54pm: "Champions don't sleep."

Steve, 11:56pm: "We're not champions. We're joint sixth."

Dave, 11:58am: "We could be tournament champions."

Mike, 12:01am: "We could also be first-round exits."

Rich, 12:03am: "Not with that attitude."

Steve, 12:05am: "I'm going to sleep. Some of us have work tomorrow."

Rich, 12:07am: "Sleep is for the weak."

Dave, 12:09am: "Sleep is for people who aren't obsessed."

Mike, 12:11am: "So none of us then."

The tournament loomed. Five weeks became four. Four became three. Three became two.

They practiced serves until Mike's shoulder hurt. Did positioning drills until Steve threatened mutiny. Analyzed match footage until Dave's eyes hurt.

"You're obsessing again," Sarah observed.

"Tournament preparation."

"You've created six new spreadsheet tabs."

"Analysis is important."

"Dave. It's a local tournament. At a leisure centre. In December."

"It's our Wimbledon." ,

"It's really not."

"It's our Wimbledon," Dave repeated firmly.

By the week of the tournament, Dave was barely sleeping. Kept thinking about draws and matchups and strategies. About serves and returns and court positioning.

"You look terrible," Priya said at work.

"Tournament this weekend."

"The Padel thing?"

"It's not a thing. It's a tournament."

"Right. Sorry. The Padel tournament thing."

"We've been training for five weeks."

"For a local tournament?"

"For our Wimbledon."

"It's not Wimbledon."

"Everyone keeps saying that."

"Because it's true."

Wednesday training session, three days before the tournament, was intense. They drilled everything. Serves. Returns. Positioning. Communication. Every scenario Dave's spreadsheet had identified as potentially crucial.

"I think we're ready," Rich said afterwards.

"Are we though?" Steve asked.

"We're as ready as we're going to be."

"That's not reassuring."

"It's realistic."

They stood in the changing room, four men who'd started this journey ten months ago as complete beginners. Who'd improved and trained and obsessed and created spreadsheets and set midnight alarms.

Who'd become actual friends.

"Whatever happens Saturday," Mike said, "it's been good. This whole thing. The training. The league. The obsession."

"Even the spreadsheets?" Steve asked.

"Especially the spreadsheets."

"I've made fifty-four tabs," Dave admitted.

"That's concerning."

"That's commitment."

"Same thing really."

Friday night, Dave couldn't sleep. Lay awake thinking about the tournament. About potential matchups. About serves and returns and everything that could go right or wrong.

"Dave," Sarah murmured. "Stop thinking."

"I'm not thinking."

"Your brain is very loud."

"Tournament's tomorrow."

"I know."

"What if we lose first round?"

"Then you lose first round."

"But we've trained for five weeks."

"Dave. Listen to me. Tomorrow you're going to play Padel. With your friends. At a local tournament. You'll probably lose. Maybe not first round. Maybe second. But you'll lose. Because you're not professional players. You're four middle-aged men who've been playing for less than a year."

"We're joint sixth."

"Out of twelve teams in a beginners' league. That's not an achievement that suggests tournament victory."

"We've improved though."

"You have. Massively. But you're still not going to win a tournament."

Dave knew she was right. Knew they'd probably lose early. Knew this wasn't actually their Wimbledon.

"But what if we do win?" he said quietly.

"Then I'll be thrilled. And surprised. And very impressed."

"But you don't think we will."

"I think you'll give it everything. I think you'll play well. I think you'll have fun. And I think you'll probably lose to someone significantly better."

"That's pessimistic."

"That's realistic."

"Can't it be both?"

"With you? Absolutely."

Saturday morning arrived. December 21st. The shortest day of the year. The winter solstice.

Their Wimbledon.

Probably.

Dave arrived at ActiveLife at 8:30am for a 10am start. So did Mike. And Steve. And Rich.

"We're all early," Mike observed.

"Apparently it's important," Steve said.

"It's very important," Rich corrected.

The tournament bracket was posted outside Court 1. Sixteen pairs. Knockout format. Quarter-finals, semi-finals, final.

Dave studied it. Their first match was against "The Net Results" - a team they'd played in league. Lost to. Badly.

"Oh good," Mike said, reading over his shoulder. "An easy first round."

"That's sarcasm, right?"

"Very much sarcasm."

They warmed up. Practiced serves. Did positioning drills. Tried to stay calm.

"How do you feel?" Rich asked.

"Terrified," Dave admitted.

"Good. Me too."

"That's not reassuring."

"It's honest."

10am arrived. The first matches began. Court 1. Dave and Rich vs The Net Results.

They walked onto court. Shook hands. Took positions.

Dave served first.

His hand was shaking.

The ball went over. Just. Barely. But over.

The Net Results returned it. Hard and low. Dave positioned himself. Saw it coming. Swung—

Perfect contact. Right down the middle. They couldn't return it.

1-0.

"YES!" Rich shouted.

They'd scored first. In a tournament. Against a team that had demolished them in league.

The match continued. They were focused. Communicating. Playing like an actual team.

They lost.

11-7.

But 11-7 was respectable. 11-7 was competitive. 11-7 was progress.

Mike and Steve played next. Against a team called "Smash and Grab."

They lost 11-5.

Both pairs eliminated first round.

Tournament over.

They gathered on the bench outside Court 1, watching other matches continue.

"Well," Steve said eventually. "That was brief."

"Very brief," Mike agreed.

"We lasted..." Rich checked his watch. "Forty-seven minutes total."

"That's not very long," Dave said.

"No."

They sat in silence. Four middle-aged men who'd trained for five weeks, created countless spreadsheets, obsessed over every detail.

Eliminated first round.

"Should we go?" Steve asked.

"Go where?" Rich said.

"I don't know. Home? Pub? Anywhere but here watching other people play?"

They looked at each other.

"Let's watch the next match," Dave said. "See how far Net Results get."

"Why?"

"Curiosity. Plus we've got nothing else to do."

So they watched. The Net Results won their second match. Then their quarter-final. Made it to the semi-finals.

"They're actually good," Mike observed.

"Or we made them look good," Steve suggested.

"We were competitive though," Rich said. "11-7. That's not embarrassing."

"It's not winning."

"No. But it's not humiliating either."

They watched the final. Two teams they'd never played. Both significantly better than anyone in the beginners' league.

"We were never going to win this," Dave said.

"No," Mike agreed.

"But we trained for five weeks like we might."

"We did."

"Was that stupid?"

"Probably."

"But worth it?"

They thought about this. About five weeks of focused training. About improvement and dedication and caring about something enough to create fifty-four spreadsheet tabs.

"Yeah," Rich said. "Worth it."

"Definitely worth it," Steve agreed.

"The training made us better," Mike added. "Even if we lost first round."

Dave nodded. Sarah had been right. They'd lost early. To someone better. Exactly as predicted.

But the five weeks of training had been good. Had been meaningful. Had been time spent with friends working toward something.

Even if that something was losing first round in a local tournament.

The prize presentation happened at noon. The winning team got a trophy. An actual trophy. Small, but real.

"Next year," Rich said, watching them lift it.

"Next year what?" Steve asked.

"Next year we win that."

"Rich. We lost first round."

"This year we lost first round. Next year is different."

"How?"

"We'll train more. Prepare better. Improve."

"We're already training three times a week."

"We could do four again."

They all looked at Dave.

"I'm doing three," Dave said firmly. "Family commitments."

"Fair," Rich said. "Three times a week. But focused. Dedicated. Tournament-specific training."

"It's December. Next tournament is probably six months away."

"Then we have six months to prepare."

"You're insane," Steve said.

"We all are," Mike corrected. "That's why we're here."

They left ActiveLife at 12:30pm. Tournament over. Season effectively done. Christmas approaching.

"Pub?" Rich suggested.

"Obviously," they all said.

At the pub, over pints and packets of crisps, they dissected the tournament. Every point. Every shot. Every decision.

"My serve was off," Dave said.

"Your serve was fine," Mike corrected. "My returns were the problem."

"Both your returns were fine," Steve said. "Their positioning was just better."

"They've probably been playing for years," Rich added.

"And we've been playing for ten months."

"Exactly."

They drank. Discussed. Analyzed. Did all the things they always did.

"Same time next week?" Rich asked eventually.

"Wednesday?" Mike confirmed.

"Wednesday."

"And Saturday?"

"Saturday."

"And Sunday?"

"Sunday."

They looked at Dave.

"Wednesday and Saturday," Dave said. "Sunday is family time now."

"Fair enough," Rich said. "Wednesday and Saturday it is."

Dave drove home at 3pm, slightly drunk, eliminated first round, feeling oddly content.

Sarah was in the garden despite the December cold, Christmas lights half-strung on the fence.

"How did it go?"

"Lost first round."

"Sorry."

"Don't be. We were competitive. 11-7. Against a team that eventually made the semi-finals."

"So moral victory?"

"Exactly."

"That's very you."

"Is it?"

"Finding the positive in losing. Making it about progress and improvement and learning opportunities."

"That's bad?"

"That's very you. Which is fine. As long as you remember it was just a local tournament."

"Our Wimbledon."

"Dave."

"Our small, local, beginners' Wimbledon."

"Better."

He helped her with the Christmas lights. Actually helped, not just stood there thinking about Padel. Strung lights. Tested bulbs. Made suggestions about placement.

"This is nice," Sarah said.

"What is?"

"You. Being present. Actually here."

"I'm always here."

"You're physically here. But mentally you're usually in a glass cage."

"Not right now."

"Not right now," Sarah agreed. "That's progress."

They finished the lights. Stepped back. Admired their work.

"They're wonky," Dave said.

"They're perfect."

"They're objectively wonky."

"They're perfectly wonky."

His phone buzzed. WhatsApp. The group discussing the tournament. Analyzing. Planning for next year.

Dave checked it. Read the messages. Didn't reply.

"You can reply," Sarah said.

"I'm being present."

"You can be present and still reply to your friends."

"Balance is hard."

"Balance is always hard."

Dave typed a quick message: "Good tournament. Proud of us. See you Wednesday."

Put his phone away.

Went inside to help Sarah with dinner.

Actually helped, not just stood in the kitchen thinking about serves and returns and court positioning.

Progress.

Balance.

Present.

Probably.

That evening, Tom came down for dinner. They talked about his architecture course. About Christmas plans. About Emily coming home from university next week.

Normal family conversation.

No Padel talk.

Well. Minimal Padel talk.

Dave mentioned the tournament once. Tom asked polite questions. Dave answered briefly. Moved on.

"Dad," Tom said as they were clearing plates.

"Yeah?"

"You're doing better."

"At what?"

"At being here. At being Dad instead of Padel Dad."

"Padel Dad?"

"You know what I mean."

Dave did know. Knew he'd been Padel Dad for months. Obsessed Dad. Absent Dad who was physically present but mentally elsewhere.

"I'm trying," Dave said.

"I can tell. It's good."

After dinner, Dave had an hour before bed. An hour he would normally spend watching YouTube videos or updating spreadsheets or analyzing match footage.

He watched a Christmas film with Sarah instead.

Well. He watched most of it. His mind wandered a few times. Thought about the tournament. About their 11-7 loss. About what they could improve for next time.

But he watched most of it.

Progress.

In bed, Sarah asked: "Disappointed about today?"

"Bit."

"Very disappointed?"

"Less than I expected to be."

"Why?"

"Because we were competitive. Because we tried. Because we've improved so much in ten months. Because..." Dave paused. "Because it was fun. Even losing first round. It was fun."

"That's growth."

"Is it?"

"Finding joy in the process instead of just the outcome? That's definitely growth."

"Huh."

"Very articulate."

"I contain multitudes."

They lay in the dark. Dave's phone buzzed once. What-sApp. Probably Rich planning next week's training. Or Mike sending a video. Or Steve making a joke about their first-round exit.

Dave didn't check it.

Checked it at 6:47am the next morning.

Obviously.

But he'd made it through the night.

Baby steps.

Progress.

Balance.

It was working.

Sort of.

Mostly.

Good enough.

Probably.

Chapter Fourteen
Christmas Day

Christmas morning, exactly one year later.

Dave woke at 7:23am - late by his recent standards - to the sound of Tom and Emily arguing downstairs about who got the good mug.

Some things never changed.

He lay in bed for a moment, Sarah still asleep beside him, and thought about the previous Christmas. About the voucher. About Googling "what is Padel" at 11pm. About having absolutely no idea what he was starting.

Twelve months ago, Padel hadn't existed in his life.

Now it was... well, not everything. But a significant part of everything.

"You're thinking about Padel," Sarah murmured, eyes still closed.

"How did you know?"

"You get a specific expression. Slightly vacant. Like you're mentally serving."

"I wasn't mentally serving."

"Were you though?"

"Maybe a bit."

She rolled over, opened her eyes. "Merry Christmas."

"Merry Christmas."

"One year."

"One year."

"How do you feel?"

Dave thought about this. About midnight bookings and spreadsheets and YouTube videos at 2am. About injuries and league matches and tournament losses. About Rich and Mike and Steve. About becoming someone who set alarms and created forty-seven-tab spreadsheets and dreamed about court positioning.

"Different," he said. "Good different. Mostly."

"Mostly?"

"I'm more obsessed than I'd like to be. More absent than I should be. More consumed by something that ultimately doesn't matter."

"But happy?"

"But happy."

Sarah kissed his forehead. "Then I suppose that's what counts."

Downstairs was chaos. Tom and Emily squabbling. Dave's mum already in the kitchen making tea nobody had asked for. Sarah's sister Linda arriving with Rob, who immediately started talking about Padel.

"Dave! How's the season going? I saw on Facebook you made joint sixth!"

"We finished sixth. Out of twelve."

"That's brilliant! I'm still playing twice a week. Got a new paddle. Carbon fiber face, EVA foam core—"

"Rob," Linda interrupted. "Not everyone wants to hear about paddles at 8am on Christmas morning."

"Dave does!"

Dave did. Absolutely did. Could have discussed paddle specifications for the next three hours.

"Maybe later," he said, catching Sarah's eye.

"After presents?" Rob suggested hopefully.

"After presents."

They gathered in the living room. The tree was slightly wonky - Sarah had insisted Dave help put it up and Dave's perfectionism had been overruled by Sarah's "it's fine, it doesn't need to be mathematically perfect."

Presents were distributed. Tom got books. Emily got clothes. Sarah got the earrings she'd specifically pointed out seventeen times. Dave's mum got a cardigan she'd definitely never wear but would insist was lovely.

And Dave got a small wrapped box from Sarah.

"This isn't..." he started.

"Open it."

Inside was a membership card. Not for ActiveLife. For a Padel club in town Dave had mentioned exactly once, three months ago.

"It's got three indoor courts," Sarah said. "Better facilities than ActiveLife. More court availability. They do open play sessions on Tuesday evenings."

"Tuesday evenings?"

"You've been talking about wanting a fourth session. But not wanting to miss Sunday family time. So. Tuesday evenings. With my blessing."

Dave stared at the membership card. "You're encouraging me to play more?"

"I'm acknowledging that this makes you happy. And that three sessions a week was probably unrealistic for someone as obsessed as you are."

"I can stick to three—"

"Dave. You've been miserable on Tuesdays. I can tell. You're home but you're not really home. You're thinking about Padel. Might as well actually be playing Padel."

"But I promised—"

"You promised to be more present. Which you have been. Significantly. This year you actually watched Emily's Christmas play."

"I always watch Emily's Christmas play."

"Last year you spent the interval checking court availability on your phone."

This was unfortunately accurate.

"Four sessions seems excessive," Dave said.

"Four sessions is excessive. But it's what you want. And it's Christmas. So. Four sessions."

Dave looked at the membership card. At Sarah's gift. At her understanding that balance didn't mean giving up completely. Just meant trying.

"Thank you," he said.

"You're welcome. Now go call your Padel friends and tell them you've joined another club. I know you want to."

"It's 9am on Christmas morning."

"Dave. Call them."

He called them.

They were thrilled.

Rich, 9:23am: "Another club! Excellent! Better facilities?"

Dave, 9:24am: "Three courts. Air conditioning. Café."

Mike, 9:26am: "Are we all joining?"

Rich, 9:27am: "Obviously."

Steve, 9:29am: "Absolutely not. I can barely afford ActiveLife."

Rich, 9:31am: "Steve mate—"

Steve, 9:32am: "Don't. We've had this conversation. I'm fine at ActiveLife."

Dave, 9:34am: "They do Tuesday evening open play. Anyone can turn up. No membership needed."

Steve, 9:36am: "Oh. That's different."

Mike, 9:38am: "So we're doing Tuesdays now?"

Rich, 9:40am: "Apparently."

Dave, 9:42am: "Just trialing it. Seeing if four sessions works."

Mike, 9:44am: "It won't work. But we'll do it anyway."

Steve, 9:46am: "That's the Padel way."

Sarah appeared in the doorway. "You called them."

"You told me to."

"I was being sarcastic."

"Were you though?"

"No. Not really."

Dave put his phone away. Helped with Christmas lunch preparation. Actually helped - chopping vegetables, stirring gravy, not just standing in the kitchen thinking about serves.

Progress.

Rob found him in the kitchen at 11:30am.

"So. Padel. How's it really going?"

Dave thought about this. How was it really going?

"Good," he said. "Really good. We finished sixth in the league. Lost first round in the winter tournament. Play three times a week. Sometimes four now apparently."

"That's commitment."

"That's obsession."

"Same thing."

"Everyone keeps saying that."

"Because it's true. You either care completely or not at all. There's no middle ground."

Dave stirred gravy. "Is that healthy?"

"Probably not. But it's better than not caring about anything at all."

"I suppose."

"You seem different," Rob said. "Than last year. More... engaged. Like you're actually living instead of just existing."

"That's dramatic."

"Is it? Last Christmas you looked tired. Worn down. Like you were going through motions. This year you look alive. Annoying and obsessed, but alive."

Dave hadn't thought about it that way. But Rob was right. Last Christmas he'd been... fine. Job was fine. Family was fine. Life was fine.

Nothing terrible. But nothing exciting either.

Just fine.

"This year is better," Dave admitted.

"Because of Padel?"

"Because of... having something. Something that's mine. That I care about. That makes me set alarms and create spreadsheets and bore people at parties."

"You bore people at parties?"

"Apparently."

"Good. Everyone should have something they're boring about."

Lunch was chaotic. Too much food. Too many people. Dave's mum complaining the turkey was dry (it wasn't). Tom and Emily arguing about Brexit (neither really cared). Rob trying to talk about Padel (everyone politely changing the subject).

Normal Christmas chaos.

But Dave was present for it. Actually there. Not thinking about court bookings or serve technique or league standings.

Well. Not constantly thinking about them.

Progress.

After lunch, while everyone was in food comas, Dave's phone buzzed.

WhatsApp group. Not Padel Lads. A different one.

Family group chat. Tom had created it last month.

Tom, 3:47pm: "Dad's being suspiciously present today."

Emily, 3:49pm: "I noticed. He's barely checked his phone."

Sarah, 3:51pm: "Christmas miracle."

Tom, 3:53pm: "Or he's sick."

Dave, 3:55pm: "I can see these messages. You know that, right?"

Emily, 3:56pm: "We know. Just keeping you accountable."

Tom, 3:58pm: "Also we're proud of you."

Dave, 4:00pm: "For being present on Christmas?"

Emily, 4:01pm: "For trying. For being better than last year."

Tom, 4:03pm: "Last year you left lunch early to watch Padel videos."

Dave, 4:05pm: "I did?"

Sarah, 4:06pm: "You absolutely did. You claimed you needed to make a work call."

Dave, 4:08pm: "Oh. Right. Sorry about that."

Tom, 4:10pm: "Point is, this year is better."

Emily, 4:11pm: "Still obsessed. But better."

Dave, 4:13pm: "I'll take it."

Evening came. Rob and Linda left. Dave's mum went for a nap. Tom and Emily disappeared upstairs to call their respective partners.

Dave and Sarah sat in the living room, Quality Street tin between them, Christmas film playing on TV that neither was really watching.

"Year in review?" Sarah said.

"Is this a performance evaluation?"

"Call it a reflection."

"Okay. Reflections. I joined a sport. Got obsessed. Created spreadsheets. Set midnight alarms. Neglected my family. Got injured. Lost tournaments. Finished joint sixth. Made friends. Found purpose. Tried to balance. Mostly failed. Sometimes succeeded."

"That's comprehensive."

"I'm very thorough."

"What about next year?"

Dave thought about this. About the new club membership. About Tuesday evenings. About Rich already planning for next season's league. About Mike researching summer tournaments. About Steve's quiet dedication to something that gave him friends.

"More of the same," Dave said. "But better at the balance part. Probably. Hopefully."

"Specific goals?"

"Don't miss important family events. Actually watch Tom's presentations. Help with Emily's dissertation. Be present for dinners. Stop checking my phone at midnight."

"Check it at 6:47am instead?"

"Baby steps."

Sarah laughed. "You're impossible."

"I know."

"But you're trying."

"I am trying."

"Then that's enough."

They sat in comfortable silence. The Christmas film reached its predictable conclusion. Everyone was happy. Everything was resolved. The good guys won.

"Do you think we'll ever win anything?" Dave asked.

"At Padel?"

"Yeah."

"Do you care?"

Dave thought about this. Did he care? They'd finished sixth. Lost first round in the tournament. Had a losing record overall.

But they'd improved. Made friends. Found something to care about.

"Not really," he said. "Winning would be nice. But that's not really the point anymore."

"What is the point?"

"Having something. Caring about something. Being part of something. Having mates who understand why you set midnight alarms and create fifty-seven spreadsheet tabs."

"Fifty-seven?"

"I added three more. Tournament analysis."

"Of course you did."

His phone buzzed. WhatsApp. Padel Lads.

Rich, 8:47pm: "Merry Christmas, lads. Been a good year."

Mike, 8:52pm: "Best year in ages."

Steve, 8:56pm: "Can't believe we finished sixth."

Rich, 9:01pm: "Joint sixth."

Steve, 9:03pm: "Still counts."

Dave, 9:05pm: "Next year we'll be joint fifth."

Mike, 9:07pm: "Aim high."

Rich, 9:09pm: "Training starts next week."

Steve, 9:11pm: "It's Christmas, Rich."

Rich, 9:13pm: "Champions don't take breaks."

Mike, 9:15pm: "We're not champions. We're joint sixth."

Rich, 9:17pm: "Not with that attitude."

Dave smiled. Put his phone down. Turned to Sarah.

"They want to start training next week."

"Of course they do."

"I said yes."

"Of course you did."

"Is that okay?"

"Dave. It's who you are now. Padel Dad. Spreadsheet Dad. Midnight Booking Dad."

"That's a lot of Dads."

"You contain multitudes."

"Everyone keeps saying that."

They finished the Quality Street. Put the tin aside. Turned off the TV.

Upstairs, getting ready for bed, Dave caught his reflection in the mirror.

Forty-eight years old. Slightly greyer than last year. Slightly more tired-looking. But somehow... lighter. More present. More alive.

Padel had done that.

Ridiculous, obsessive, spreadsheet-generating, midnight-alarm-setting Padel.

In bed, Sarah asked: "Any regrets?"

"About Padel?"

"About the year. About the obsession. About any of it."

Dave thought about missed presentations and neglected family dinners and months of being mentally elsewhere. About injuries and losses and first-round tournament exits.

About Rich and Mike and Steve. About having mates. About caring about something enough to bore people at parties.

"No," he said. "No regrets."

"Even the bad parts?"

"Even the bad parts. They led to the good parts."

"That's very philosophical."

"I'm very deep."

"You're very something."

They lay in the dark, Sarah's breathing evening out as she fell asleep.

Dave's phone buzzed on the bedside table.

He didn't check it.

Well. He thought about checking it. Hand actually reached toward it.

But he didn't check it.

Progress.

Would check it at 6:47am tomorrow.

Obviously.

But tonight, on Christmas Day, exactly one year after receiving a voucher that changed everything, Dave left his phone unchecked.

Closed his eyes.

Thought about Padel.

Obviously.

About serves and returns and court positioning and league tables and tournament brackets and everything that had consumed his life for twelve months.

But also about family. About Tom and Emily and Sarah. About being present. About balance.

About being someone who cared about something. Who set alarms and created spreadsheets and generally lost his mind over a sport played in a glass cage.

About being ridiculous.

About being happy.

About being alive.

His last thought before falling asleep was about Tuesday evening sessions at the new club.

His last feeling was contentment.

His last action was not checking his phone.

Two out of three wasn't bad.

Progress.

Balance.

Life.

Good life, actually.

Really quite good.

Despite everything.

Because of everything.

Thanks to a £20 voucher and a ridiculous Spanish sport and three men who became friends.

Thanks to Padel.

Thanks to obsession.

Thanks to spreadsheets and midnight alarms and fifty-seven tabs and everything else that normal people would consider completely insane.

Dave fell asleep smiling.

Dreaming about Padel.

Obviously.

But this time, also dreaming about Christmas dinner and family movie nights and Tom's presentations and Emily's plays and Sarah's tolerance and everything else that mattered.

Balance.

Finally.

Sort of.

Mostly.

Good enough.

Definitely good enough.

At 6:47am on Boxing Day, Dave woke naturally.

Checked his phone.

The group chat had exploded overnight.

Forty-three messages about training schedules and tournament dates and next season's goals.

Dave read them all.

Smiled.

Replied: "See you Wednesday."

Put his phone down.

Got up.

Made coffee.

Started his day.

His Padel day.

His normal day.

His perfectly balanced, slightly obsessed, generally ridiculous day.

And it was good.

Really, really good.

Better than good, actually.

It was everything.

Well. Not everything.

But enough.

More than enough.

Exactly right.

Probably.

Printed in Dunstable, United Kingdom